Jayden

GRADED
ENGLISH GRAMMAR
(INTERNATIONAL EDITION)
Book - 8

By

Ms. LATA SETH

(M. A. Delhi University)

DREAMLAND PUBLICATIONS

J-128, KIRTI NAGAR, NEW DELHI - 110 015 (INDIA)
Ph. : 011-2543 5657, 2510 6050 Fax. : 011-2543 8283
E-mail : dreamland@vsnl.com
www.dreamlandpublications.com

Published in 2013 by
DREAMLAND PUBLICATIONS
J-128, Kirti Nagar, New Delhi - 110 015 (India)
Tel : 011-2510 6050, Fax : 011-2543 8283
E-mail : dreamland@vsnl.com, www.dreamlandpublications.com
Copyright © 2013 Dreamland Publications
All rights reserved. No part of this publication should be reproduced, stored in a retrieval system or transmitted in any form or by any means—electronic, mechanical, photocopying, recording or otherwise—without the prior permission of Dreamland Publications.
ISBN 978-17-3014-140-9

Printed by : RAVE INDIA

PREFACE

This edition of English Grammar caters to the needs of pupils of Primary and Middle grades. It has been presented in a unique manner and in a style that is quite off the beaten track to derive maximum benefit for the users of this book.

The present book is meant for the pupils of Grade VIII who have studied the first seven books of the series. The first five books in the series emphasized the study of English Grammar in elementary form with the aim of allowing the users to master the fundamental of the language. The sixth and seventh book of the series reiterated the usage to a more refined level.

This book deals mainly with the important facts related to Nouns, Pronouns, Adjectives, Adverbs, Prepositions and Conjunctions. The book also contains exclusive chapters on Speech — Direct and Indirect.

A Comprehensive Vocabulary and Written Composition are other features of this book. The study of this book will prepare the learner for the study of higher structural aspects of English language.

Illustrations have been used as a potent medium to teach children the facts on English Grammar. Efforts have been taken to keep the lessons simple and interesting.

It is hoped that this book will be adequately supported by the teaching fraternity. It is believed that the book will serve the purpose meant for, as it is much superior to similar books available. Suggestions for improvement shall be deeply acknowledged for inclusion in future editions.

—Ms. LATA SETH

CONTENTS

1. Kinds of Simple Sentences 5
2. Transformation of Simple Sentences 10
3. Nouns : Important Facts 17
4. Pronouns : Important Facts 25
5. Adjectives : Important Facts 34
6. Adverbs : Important Facts 46
7. Prepositions : Important Facts 58
8. Conjunctions : Important Facts 65
9. Speech—Direct and Indirect – I 68
10. Speech—Direct and Indirect – II 80
11. Speech—Direct and Indirect – III 86
12. Speech—Direct and Indirect – IV 92
13. Speech—Direct and Indirect – V .. 100
14. Speech—Direct and Indirect – VI 108
15. Punctuation – I 113
16. Punctuation – II 122
17. Analysis of Sentences 129
18. Synthesis of Sentences 136
19. Rules of Agreement 144
20. Grammatical Errors 147
21. Figures of Speech 154
22. Vocabulary 156
23. Written Composition 184
24. Paraphrasing 186
25. Comprehension 188
26. Summarizing 193
27. Picture Composition 197
28. Writing Stories 200
29. Writing Essays 205
30. Writing Dialogues 210
31. Writing Letters 213

1 KINDS OF SIMPLE SENTENCES

We read about five kinds of sentences in the previous book. These kinds are :
1. Statements or Assertive Sentences
2. Questions or Interrogative Sentences
3. Commands or Imperative Sentences
4. Wishes or Optative Sentences
5. Exclamations or Exclamatory Sentences

We know many important facts about these various kinds of sentences. Let us review these facts.

1. ASSERTIVE SENTENCES

(a) **Assertive sentences express *facts, actions* and *happenings*.**
(b) Assertive sentences can be affirmative or negative.
(c) An assertive sentence always ends with a **full stop (.)**.

Examples : (a) The fox **is** a cunning animal.   (*Affirmative fact*)
(b) The hare **is not** a cunning animal   (*Negative fact*)
(c) The tortoise **beat** the hare in a race.   (*Affirmative action*)
(d) The tortoise **did not lose** the race.   (*Negative action*)
(e) Cholera **has broken out** in the city. (*Affirmative happening*)
(f) There **was no** snowfall at night.   (*Negative happening*)

2. INTERROGATIVE SENTENCES

(a) **Interrogative sentences are of two types :**
   1. Those beginning with *helping verbs*
   2. Those beginning with *question-words*
(b) Interrogative sentences beginning with helping verbs are answered using yes or no.
(c) Interrogative sentences beginning with question-words are answered directly through statements.
(d) An interrogative sentence always ends in a **question mark (?)**.

Examples : (a) 1. **Do** you like reading stories ? ⎤
2. **Has** the prayer bell gone ? ⎥ *Questions beginning with helping verbs*
3. **Are** you ready to help me ? ⎦

5

(b) 1. **What** made you laugh so loudly ? ⎫ *Questions*
    2. **How** are you feeling now ? ⎬ *beginning with*
    3. **Why** have you come so late? ⎭ *helping verbs*

IMPERATIVE SENTENCES

(a) Imperative sentences express *commands*, *requests*, *pieces of advice* and *proposals*.
(b) Imperative sentences do not begin with any subject. The subject **you** remains unstated but *understood* in these sentences.
(c) Affirmative imperative sentences begin with the **base form of a verb.**
(d) Negative imperative sentences begin with **do not** or **never**.
(e) There are no interrogative forms of imperative sentences.
(f) An imperative sentence always ends with a **full stop (.)**.

Examples :
1. (a) **Do** it right now and here. ⎫ **COMMANDS**
   (b) **Never** do it again. ⎭ *Positive, negative*
2. (a) **Give** me something to eat, please. ⎫ **REQUESTS**
   (b) **Do not** kill me, Your Majesty. ⎭ *Positive, negative*
3. (a) Always **respect** your elders. ⎫ **ADVICE**
   (b) **Never** tell a lie. ⎭ *Positive, negative*
4. (a) **Let us go** boating in the river. ⎫ **PROPOSALS**
   (b) **Let not** the thief **run** away. ⎭ *Positive, negative*

OPTATIVE SENTENCES

(a) Optative sentences express *wishes*, *prayers*, *blessings* and *curses*.
(b) There are no interrogative forms of optative sentences.
(c) An optative sentence always ends in an **exclamation mark (!)**.

Eamples :
1. **If only** I were a king !   (*wish*)
2. **May** you live long !   (*blessing*)
3. **May** God grant you all His gifts !   (*prayer*)
4. **May** you be doomed, O tyrant !   (*curse*)

5. EXCLAMATORY SENTENCES

(a) Exclamatory sentences are exclaimed *in part* or *in full* under the effect of *sudden strong emotions*.

(b) An exclamatory sentence always ends in an **exclamation mark** (!).
(c) While taking an exclamatory form, a sentence loses its interrogative structure and becomes more or less an *assertive sentence* ; as—

How beautiful is the butterfly ?   (interrogative)
How beautiful the butterfly is !   (exclamatory)
What nonsense is it ?   (interrogative)
What nonsense it is !   (exclamatory)

TEST YOURSELF

A. Arrange each set of jumbled words into an *assertive sentence* :

1. this hear was to she news shocked sad
   ....
2. ball not the round earth like is a
   ....
3. noodles very seem be you of to fond
   ....
4. out has famine in a town our broken
   ....
5. felt axe woodman sad to very his lose the
   ....
6. spherical the is shape in earth
   ....
7. not it did at yesterday rain all
   ....

B. Arrange each set of jumbled words into an *interrogative sentence*:

1. you me are with why displeased
   ....
2. orange the isn't an round earth like
   ....
3. Japan the of best our land isn't motherland all
   ....

4. friend whom my see want to you do
   ....

5. watch is by time your what it
   ....

6. our needs three which chief are basic
   ....

7. closed shall school the remain tomorrow
   ....

C. Arrange each set of jumbled words into an *imperative sentence* :

1. leave your do finish room the not you classwork till
   ....

2. the give of habit up lies once telling for all
   ....

3. swimming the go river us in let
   ....

4. peace and in others live let in live too peace
   ....

5. eat kindly to me give something.
   ....

6. take is never yours not what.
   ....

7. play us for time let carom some
   ....

D. Arrange each set of jumbled words into an *optative sentence*:

1. best the enjoy of you health may your
   ....

2. were would man that a I rich
   ....

3. shower on gifts His you may all God
   ....

4. down O with tyrant you
   ....

E. Arrange each set of jumbled words into an *exclamatory sentence* :

1. fine how the weather is
   ....
2. wonderful wow what movie a it was
   ....
3. are alas all undone we
   ....
4. captured the hurrah enemy have post we
   ....
5. suggested silly a what you plan have
   ....
6. forceful a what hit indeed
   ....

F. Write the correct ending *punctuation mark* for each type of sentences :

1. Exclamatory Sentences .... 2. Positive Statements ....
3. Imperative Sentences .... 4. Interrogative Sentences ....
5. Optative Sentences .... 6. Negative Statements............

G. Name :

(a) two types of assertive sentences : ....
(b) two types of interrogative sentences : ....
(c) four things that imperative sentences express :
    ....
(d) four things that optative sentences express :
    ....
(c) eight common emotions that exclamatory sentences express :
    ....
    ....

2 TRANSFORMATION OF SIMPLE SENTENCES

We read about **five kinds** of simple sentences in the previous chapter. They are :
1. Statements or Assertive Sentences
2. Questions or Interrogative Sentences
3. Commands or Imperative Sentences
4. Wishes or Optative Sentences
5. Exclamations or Exclamatory Sentences

These sentences can be changed, *i.e.* transformed from one kind to another *without any change in meaning*. This is called **Transformation of Sentences**. Let us study it in detail.

FROM STATEMENTS TO QUESTIONS

Questions are used not only for enquiring about something but also for **suggesting an answer** that the speaker himself desires to be given.

Observe the following examples :

1. A cow cannot change its colour. *(Statement)*
   Can a cow *change* its colour ? *(Interrogative)*
2. Everyone wants to live freely. *(Statement)*
   Who does not want to live freely ? *(Interrogative)*
3. Nobody can take such an insult. *(Statement)*
   Who can take such an insult ? *(Interrogative)*

QUESTIONS TO STATEMENTS

Observe the following examples :
1. If you slap me, shall I not weep ? *(Interrogative)*
   I shall certainly weep if you slap me. *(Statement)*
2. Who is so mean that will not love his/her motherland ? *(Interrogative)*
   Nobody is so mean that will not love his/her motherland. *(Statement)*
3. Why are you silent today, O great man ? *(Interrogative)*
   You must not be silent today, O great man. *(Statement)*

FROM NEGATIVE TO AFFIRMATIVE

Observe the following examples :
1. His timely help *cannot be forgotten*. *(Negative)*

His timely help *is unforgettable*. (Affirmative)
2. An honest man *will never* take such a step. (Negative)
   An honest man *will* keep away from such a step. (Affirmative)
3. *No sooner did he see me* than he ran away. (Negative)
   As soon as he saw me, he ran away (Affirmative)
4. *None* but the brave *deserves* the best. (Negative)
   Only the brave *deserve* the best. (Affirmative)

AFFIRMATIVE TO NEGATIVE

Observe the following examples :
1. I have *something* to say. (Affirmative)
   I have *nothing* to say. (Negative)
2. I have something to say. (Affirmative)
   I have nothing to say. (Negative)
3. Learned men *can be* unwise too. (Affirmative)
   Learned men *are not* always wise. (Negative)

TEST YOURSELF

A. **Transform each of the following sentences into its *interrogative form* :**

1. Animals and birds are also living-beings.
   ....
2. Everybody needs food, clothes and shelter.
   ....
3. I shall certainly laugh if you tickle me.
   ....
4. I will always obey my parents.
   ....
5. A lion can never give up its pride.
   ....
6. That man has no shame at all.
   ....
7. Even a little spark can kindle a terrible fire.
   ....

B. Transform each of these interrogative sentences into its *negative form* :

1. What more can I do than this for you ?
   ....
2. Who has seen such bad days before this ?
   ....
3. Can virtue be ever created by laws ?
   ....
4. Why should you poke your nose into others' affairs ?
   ....
5. Who can describe the beauty of nature ?
   ....
6. Has anyone seen a better day than this ?
   ....
7. Have you seen an aeroplane go up ?
   ....

C. Transform each of these negative sentences into its *affirmative form* :

1. A wise man will never violate moral laws.
   ....
2. None but cowards run away from the battle-field.
   ....
3. You are not taller than he is.
   ....
4. Great men do not belong to any one nation.
   ....
5. His office is not so near by from here.
   ....
6. No sooner did the teacher come than the children became silent.
   ....

7. No one can deny that you are very sincere.
   ....

D. **Transform each of the following sentences into its *negative form* :**

1. It always pours when it rains.
   ....

2. He has a good reason to make such a claim.
   ....

3. There is always some lightning in every cloud.
   ....

4. She is a lady with striking beauty.
   ....

5. A soon as the master came, everyone stood up.
   ....

7. He is quite as foolish as you are.
   ....

STATEMENTS TO EXCLAMATIONS

Observe the following examples :

1. *I wish I had never left my home.* (Statement)
   If only I had never left my home ! (Exclamation)
2. We had an extremely merry time there. (Statement)
   What a merry time we had there ! (Exclamation)
3. The mighty have fallen very low indeed. (statement)
   How low the mighty have fallen indeed ! (Exclamation)
4. The beauty of nature is immense. (Statement)
   How immense the beauty of nature is ! (Exclamation)

EXCLAMATIONS TO STATEMENTS

Observe the following examples :

1. Would that I had been a prince ! (Exclamation)
   I wish I had been a prince. (Statement)
2. What a lame excuse you are putting up ! (Exclamation)
   You are putting up a very lame excuse. (Statement)

3.	A soldier, and afraid of death !	(*Exclamation*)
	It is strange for a soldier to be afraid of death.	(*Statement*)
4.	A horse ! my kingdom for a horse !	(*Exclamation*)
	I can give away my kingdom for a horse.	(*Statement*)

SUBSTITUTING A DIFFERENT PART OF SPEECH

Observe the following examples :

1.	He *promised* to help me with money.	(*verb*)
	He gave me a *promise* of help with money.	(***noun***)
2.	Gold and silver *differ* in many ways.	(*verb*)
	Gold and silver are different in many ways.	(*adjective*)
3.	I have fixed a *meeting* with him today.	(*noun*)
	I am to *meet* him today.	(***verb***)
4.	The show gave us much *pleasure*.	(*noun*)
	We were much *pleased* to see the show.	(*verb*)
5.	He *forcibly* made his way through the crowd.	(*adverb*)
	He *forced* his way through the crowd.	(*verb*)
6.	The rain will give a *boost* to the crop.	(*noun*)'
	The rain will *boost* the crop.	(*verb*)

TEST YOURSELF

A. Rewrite each statement in the form of an *exclamation* :

1. That is a shameless fall for such a great man.
   ....
2. I wish that a desert were my dwelling place.
   ....
3. The rose flowers looked extremely lovely.
   ....
4. I earnestly desire to gain the first prize.
   ....

5. A little knowledge is really a dangerous thing.
   ....

6. I very much like to be in my native land again.
   ....

7. It is extremely shameful of you indeed.
   ....

B. Rewrite each exclamation in the form of a *statement* :

1. If only I could see my motherland again !
   ....

2. If I had not squandered my wealth !
   ....

3. How proud she is of her beautiful face !
   ....

4. What a noise they are making !
   ....

5. Well done ! my boys !
   ....

6. If only I had been there !
   ....

C. Do as directed :

(a) Use *verbs* as substitutes for words in italics :

1. He talked to me very *amusingly*.
   ....

2. He is a citizen of America *by birth*.
   ....

3. You must act according to my *advice*.
   ....

4. I will give you much *assistance* in this project.
   ....

(b) Use *nouns* as substitutes for words in italics :

1. A spider is wonderfully *intelligent*.
   ....
2. I am sorry that my son *behaved* so *rudely*.
   ....
3. I left my house at 5.00 a.m. as you *desired*.
   ....
4. He *allowed* me 40 dollars a month.
   ....
5. I *hoped* that he would mend his ways.
   ....
6. I *feared* that I would fall down.
   ....
7. We need to work hard *to be successful*.
   ....

(c) Rewrite each sentence substituting an *adjective* for the word in italics :

1. He is a man of remarkable *intelligence*.
   ....
2. At times he *acts dishonestly*.
   ....
3. *Such a crime* is punished by death.
   ....
4. A man *believing in vice* never prospers.
   ....
5. I believe that a *man of industry* must succeed.
   ....
6. A man *loving truth* is honoured everywhere.
   ....
7. Some persons are born *in poverty* while others *in richness*.
   ....

3 NOUNS: IMPORTANT FACTS

Nouns are words used to identify persons or things.
We have read about nouns and their kinds in the previous books of this series. In this chapter, we shall study nouns from the following angles :

    (*a*)   Nouns and Capital Letters
    (*b*)   Whether a noun is *singular* or *plural* in form.
    (*c*)   Whether a noun *needs a determiner* before it or not.
    (*d*)   Whether a noun needs a *singular* or a *plural* verb.
    (*e*)   Noun Substitutes
    (*f*)   Whether a noun is a male or a female.
    (*g*)   Compound Nouns
    (*h*)   Nouns that go in pairs, yet they are singular.

A. NOUNS AND CAPITAL LETTERS

Most nouns begin with small letters unless they are used to start any sentence. But the following types of nouns always have their first letters capitals.

1. **My** sister **Jennifer** is an **M.A.** in **English**.
2. **I** shall not come to office on **Monday**.
3. **He** has left for **Paris** today.
4. **Germans** are very intelligent and hard-working.
5. **She** has been learning **French** for two months.

B. COUNTABLE NOUNS

Most nouns have two forms—**singular form** and **plural form**. The singular form is used to refer to one person or thing. The plural form is used to refer to persons or things that are more than one. Such nouns can be counted. So, they are called countable nouns ; as—

    (*a*) one **book**   *five* **books**   (*b*) *one* **day**   *many* **days**
    (*c*) *an* **apple**   *six* **apples**   (*d*) *one* **minute**   *ten* **minutes**

(*a*) **A** *countable noun* has a determiner used before it when it is used in **singular form** ; as—

    1. I got into *my* **car** and started it.
    2. We left *our* **house** and went for it.

(b) **Normally *countable plural nouns* do not take determiners before them; as—**
1. Our school has large *class-rooms*.
2. Most class-rooms have *computers* also in them.

(c) **But if something special is linked with a plural noun, we use *a determiner* before it ; as—**
1. *Our* computers are of a fine quality.
2. *The* rooms in this building are not very large.

(d) You have read about singular and plural forms of nouns in the previous books of this series. But some nouns have the same form as singulars and plurals ; as—

(a) a **sheep** ; *nine* **sheep**   (b) a **fish** ; *several* **fish**
(c) a **deer** ; *nine* **deer**   (d) a **series** ; *three* **series**

Other nouns of this class are :

gallows, species, summons, innings, dice, aircraft, bison, cross-roads, crops, precis, news, spacecraft.

C. COUNTABLE NOUNS

(a) some nouns refer to things that cannot be counted. They include qualities, *processes, topics, substances etc*. Such nouns have only one form each and so they are not used with number. These nouns usually do not take *a, an,* or *the* before them ; as—

1. She is a girl with *intelligence*.   2. We need *food* and *water* to live.
3. They are talking about *religion*.   4. U.A.E. produces oil in *abundance*.

These uncountable nouns take singular verbs after them ; as

Fear is a sin while **courage** is a virtue.

(b) There are some uncountable nouns in English that refer to things but they are countable in other languages. Here is a list of such nouns :

advice	baggage	furniture	hair	homework
information	knowledge	luggage	news	machines
spaghetti	traffic	research	progress	money

(c) Some uncountable nouns end in *s* and look like plurals. But they are, in fact, singular. Here is a list of such nouns :

economics	billiards	mathematics	cards	rabies
means	politics	mechanics	darts	mumps
electronics	physics	alms	measles	diabetes

UNIQUE NOUNS

There are certain things (nouns) that are **unique**, *i.e.* they are talked about as only one. So, they are used in the *singular form*. And we know that each singular noun is always used with a *determiner*. The following nouns are *commonly used* as unique nouns and are preceded by **the** :

the sun	**the** moon	**the** sky	**the** air
the ground	**the** earth	**the** future	**the** past
the present	**the** universe	**the** world	**the** atmosphere

NOUNS ALWAYS PLURAL

There are nouns that are thought of as **plural** rather than **singular.** So, they have only plural forms. Here is a list of such commonly used nouns :

goods	clothes	premises	expenses	resources
refreshments	rains	gentry	police	vermin
compasses	dividers	looks	means	poultry
people	thanks	troops	manners	forces
remains	ashes	jeans	pants	shorts
glasses	trousers	spectacles	panties	scissors
tongs	pincers	pliers	shoes	shears

COLLECTIVE NOUNS

Many collective nouns are used in two ways to give different meanings. When they are used as a group, they take a singular verb. But when they refer to the members of the group individually, they take a plural verb. Here are a few examples :

1. (*a*) This family is not poor anymore. (*singular*)
   (*b*) This family are perfectly normal. (*plural*)

3. (a) Let me know what the enemy is planning. (*singular*)
   (b) The enemy are breaking up. (*plural*)

Given below is a list of common collective nouns :

army	audience	bacteria	board	company
committee	council	crew	data	fleet
family	jury	flock	gang	group
herd	government	media	swarm	regiment
public	staff	team		

NOUNS RARELY USED ALONE

There are nouns that need a qualifier or a modifier to give a clear meaning ; as —

circumstances	citizenship	culture	discovery
edition	impression	level	nature
position	robe	status	system

NOUNS STANDING FOR A CLASS

When we want to mention people who share the same quality or characteristics, we use an **adjective** rather than a *noun* and determiner **the** before it, as—

Instead of saying *poor people*, we say **the poor**.

Instead of saying *young people*, we say **the young**.

(a) **We never add *s* to such a noun.**

(b) **When such a noun is used it takes a *plural verb*.**

Examples : 1. The poor **are** always at the mercy of *the rich*.
2. The injured **were** taken to the hospital.

NATIONALITY NOUNS

Nationality nouns are of two types :

(a) **Those that have plurals ; as—**
   Germans, Poles, Americans, Norwegians, etc.

(b) **Those that are adjectives preceded by *the* ; as**
   the Japanese, the Chinese, the English, the French, etc.

GERUNDS

These nouns have the same form as the present participle of a verb. When this form is used to **denote an activity**, it is a *noun* and is called the **Gerund** ; as—

1. **Singing** is my hobby.
2. He likes **playing** cards.
2. **Walking** is a good exercise.
4. **Driving** needs much care.

Some gerunds nouns are :

shopping	swimming	boating	batting
bowling	angling	mountaineering	smoking
gambling	drinking	painting	drawing

COMPOUND NOUNS

Compound nouns are made of more-than-one word. The group acts as a noun. Here are some examples :

WRITTEN SEPARATE

personal computer	address book	can opener	air raid
swimming pool	race course	credit card	dining room
contact lens	fairy tale	film star	fire engine
bulletin	bird of prey	book worm	alarm clock

WRITTEN WITH A HYPHEN

baby-sitting	looker-on	letter-box	cover-up
passer-by	runner-up	T-shirt	x-ray
brother-in-law	bride-to-be	hunky-dory	pen-friend

NOUNS IN PAIRS

Some nouns go in pairs and are used as singular nouns ; as—

Bread and butter   milk and eggs   pen and paper

Examples:
1. *Bread and butter* is a perfect food.
2. The horse and carriage *is* at the door.
3. *Milk and eggs* makes a fine breakfast.

TEST YOURSELF

A. Answer the following questions :
1. What are *nouns* ?
   ....
2. Which nouns begin with a *capital letter* each ?
   ....
3. What are *countable nouns* ?
   ....
4. What are *uncountable nouns* ?
   ....
5. Which nouns are called *unique nouns* ? Give four examples.
   ....

B. Complete each statement :
1. The determiner *a* is used before each noun that begins with a .... sound.
2. The determiner *an* is used before each noun that begins with a .... sound.
3. The nouns—*news* and *politics*—are of .... number.
4. The nouns—*goods* and *people*—are of .... number.
5. *The poor* is a noun that takes a .... verb.

C. Write :
(a) five common gerunds :
   ....
(b) five nouns having the same *singular* and *plural* :
   ....
(c) five uncountable nouns :
   ....
(d) five countable nouns ending in *s* :
   ....
(e) Five nouns that are always plural :
   ....

(f) five nouns that are always singular :

....

D. Here are a few nouns. Which of them are used as singulars and which as plurals ? Indicate in the blank :

1. jeans .... 3. shorts ....
4. news .... 5. knowledge ....
6. money .... 7. thanks ....
8. shears .... 9. electronics ....
10. economics .... 11. police ....

E. The nouns given below are seldom used alone. Write a suitable word before each noun :

1. .... circumstances 2. .... culture
3. .... impression 4. .... citizenship
5. .... edition 6. .... impression
7. .... level 8. .... affairs

F. Use each of the following collective nouns both as a singular and a plural.

1. audience : (a) ....
   (b) ....
2. jury : (a) ....
   (b) ....
3. family : (a) ....
   (b) ....
4. committee : (a) ....
   (b) ....

G. Write the correct word for each group of the words :

1. a bill of five dollars = ...
2. a leave for three days = ...
3. a coin of fifty cents = ...
4. a plan for five years = ...
5. a hotel with five stars = ...
6. a rope three meters long = ...
7. an attack from three sides = ...

H. Complete each pair :

1. A....................and saucer
2. A spoon and....................
3. A....................and table
4. A husband and....................
5. A needle and....................
6. A pen....................
7. A....................and arrow
8. Rich and....................
9. A....................and fork
10. ....and butter

I. Write five *unique nouns* each along with the correct determiners :

....

J. Each of these nouns has *two meanings in its two plural* forms. Write the two different meanings :

Singular	Plural		
1. Arm	arms	1.	....
		2.	....
2. Minute	minutes	1.	....
		2.	....
3. Manner	manners	1.	....
		2.	....
4. Letter	letters	1.	....
		2.	....

4 PRONOUNS: IMPORTANT FACTS

In speech and writing, we have to refer to things (nouns) already mentioned. We can do so only by repeating those nouns. But it does not make good English. We repeat them only when it is necessary to do so. Generally we use words that are substitutes for these nouns. These substitutes are called **pronouns**.

An example will clarify the point.

1. This is a very beautiful *park*. Everyone likes to visit **this park**.
2. This is a very beautiful *park*. Everyone likes to visit **it**.

In sentence 1, the word – *park* – has been repeated but it sounds awkward.
In sentence 2, the word – *it* – has been used for the word—*park*. So, the sentence sounds well. The word – *it* – is a **pronoun**.

THE PRONOUN—YOU

Normally **you** is used for the *person* or *people* to whom one talks. But it is used to **refer to people in general** also ; as—

You can well imagine how big the Earth is.

You must endure what **you** cannot cure.

THE PRONOUN—WE

(a) In general, the pronoun–we–is used to refer to the group *that includes the speaker* ; as—

Where shall **we** meet again, Alfred ?

(b) The pronoun–we–is used for *society*, *community* or even *mankind*; as—
1. **We** are, in fact, just humans.
2. **We** can't live without air, water and food.
3. **We** are playthings in the hands of fate.

THE PRONOUN—THEY

(a) They is a third person pronoun of plural number. It refers to people or things that *do not include the speaker* and the people *who are spoken to* ; as—
1. All the people think I am a coward, don't **they**?

2. Magazines reach me as soon as **they** are published.
3. Weather conditions varied here as **they** do elsewhere.

(b) **They** is used for people in general ; as—
1. It is what **they** call love.
2. **They** say that honesty is the best policy.

(c) **They** is used to refer to those people whose identity need not be stated ; as—
1. Don't worry mother ; **they** are going to discharge you soon. (Here **they** stands for hospital authorities.)

THE PRONOUN—IT

(a) *The pronoun–it–is used to refer to something that is **not** male or female ; as—*
1. I have bought a new book. **It** contains interesting stories.
2. Have you ever been to the Taj ? Yes, **it** is a wonderful building.

(b) **It**–*is used to refer to an animal if its* **gender** *is* **unknown** *or* **unimportant** *; as—*
1. I saw a bear in the zoo. **It** had thick fur.
2. If the jackal is still around, **it** will not escape.

(c) **It** – is also used for babies when their gender is not important ; as—
The queen loved the baby but the maid hated **it**.

(d) **It** – is used to refer to *time, date, day, weather, situation* etc. ; as—

TIME	DATE
1. What time is it ?	1. What date is it ?
It is half past four.	It is the 15th.

DAY	WEATHER
1. What day is it today?	1. It is hot and stuffy.
It is Friday.	2. It is very chilly here.
2. What day was it yesterday?	3. It looks like rain.
It was Thursday.	4. It is raining heavily.
3. What day will it be tomorrow?	5. It is dry and windy.
It will be Saturday.	6. It is so pleasant and cool.

SITUATIONS

1. How calm and peaceful **it** is here!
2. **It** is so noisy and disturbing.

(e) **It** – *is used as an impersonal subject*; as—

1. **It** doesn't matter.
2. **It** is I who am at fault.
3. **It** costs nothing to laugh heartily.
4. **It** was silly of you to rebuke her like that.
5. **It** was amazing that she did not greet you even.
6. **It** looks awkward to travel with heavy luggage.

(f) **It** *is used as an* **object** *to verbs*— **like, hate** *etc.*— *to express feelings*; as—

1. I like **it** to be here. (here = **this place**)
2. I would hate **it** if you turn down my request.

Some other such verbs are : *enjoy, dislike, love, prefer, appreciate*.

(g) **It** *is used to express* **comments**; as—

1. **It** is really fun working round the clock.
2. **It** is nice to have you with us on this happy occasion.
3. **It** was a very bitter experience.
4. **It** pleases me to help you like that.
5. **It** is hard to get a sincere friend.
6. I thought **it** proper to resign immediately.

(h) **It** *is used to refer to a* **person** *with emphasis*; as—

1. **It** is *he* who called me names.
2. **It** is *we* who are to blame.
3. **It** is *they* who are spoiling the entire game.
4. **It** is the *parents* who can make a child good or bad.

(i) **It** *is used to express* **time** *or* **cost** *for a job or thing*; as—

(a)
1. **It** takes about an hour to reach the station.
2. **It** took me a year to save one thousand dollars.
3. **It** takes me twenty minutes to walk up to school from my house.

(b)
1. **It** costs nothing to remain happy.
2. **It** costs about 15 dollars to *buy* such a shirt.

(j) **It** – is used with the verbs **need, require** ; as—
1. **It** needs a lot of courage to face a tiger.
2. **It** requires a huge amount of money to start a business.

POSSESSIVE PRONOUNS

We often have to express the relationship of belonging, *i.e.* we have to indicate that something belongs to someone. For this, we have to use **Possessive Pronouns** which are only six in number as shown below :

1. *My* shirt is better than **his**.
2. Is this cup of tea **mine** or **yours** ?
3. It was our fault, not **theirs**.
4. These ideas are **ours**.
5. These books are **hers**, not **his**.

Person	Singular	Plural
First	Mine	Ours
Second	Yours	Yours
Third	His/her	Theirs

NOTE —
1. Never confuse the six possessive pronouns given in the above table with the possessive words **my, our, your, his, her, it, their**. These seven words also show possession but they are not pronouns. They are used before nouns as **determiners**.
2. Possessive pronouns come after the verbs that follow the nouns governed by the possessive pronouns.
3. **Its** is never used as a possessive pronoun. It is used as a possessive determiner only.
4. **His** – is used both as a *determiner* and as a *pronoun* ; as—
    (a)   This is **his** towel.   (determiner)
    (b)   This towel is **his**.   (pronoun)

ONE—AS A PERSONAL PRONOUN

The word—**one**—is used to **refer to people in general**.
1. **One** must do **one's** duty honestly.
2. **One** has to work hard to achieve success.
3. Both the shirts are fine. Which **one** do you like ?

REFLEXIVE PRONOUNS

These pronouns are used when the object (direct or indirect) of a verb is the same person/thing as the subject of the verb. These pronouns are used in two different ways as under :

(a)   **As** *objects* **to verbs** :
1. She stretched **herself** out on the sofa.

2. History keeps repeating **itself**.
3. The soldiers formed **themselves** into a group.
4. You must ask **yourself** what to do.
5. She stared at **herself** in the mirror.
6. What do you think of **yourself**?
7. You must feel ashamed of **yourself**.

(b) **For** *emphasis* :

1. We **ourselves** had to do this job.
2. The king **himself** rose to welcome the boy.
3. The town **itself** was very small indeed.
4. I **myself** was surprised to hear his words.

DEMONSTRATIVE PRONOUNS

There are four demonstrative pronouns only :

1. *This*   2. *These*   3. *That*   4. *Those*

The same care has to be taken while using these pronouns as you did while using possessive pronouns. More clearly—

1. If any of these four words is followed by a noun, it will not be a *pronoun*. It will become a **determiner**.
2. If any of these words stands independently for a noun, it will be a **demonstrative pronoun**.

Observe the following examples :

Pronouns
1. What is **this** ?
2. **These** are no ordinary problems.
3. **That** *seems* very interesting.
4. **Those** are quite easy questions.

Determiners
1. **This** book is mine.
2. **These** *girls* are very smart.
3. **That** *sum* is very difficult.
4. **Those** *girls* are all dancers.

RECIPROCAL PRONOUNS

There are two pronominal phrases that are called **reciprocal pronouns** because they show that **people** *do the same thing to each other, feel the same way* or *have the same* **relationship** ; as—

1. We must respect **each other**.
2. A husband and wife must understand **each other**.
3. All the workers looked at **one another**.

REMEMBER :
1. **Each** *can be used as the subject of a verb ; as—*
    (a) Here are two cocks. **Each** is looking at the other.
    (b) Two cranes are fighting. **Each** is trying to seize the other's neck.
2. **Each,** *when followed by a noun, becomes a determiner ; as—*
    (a) **Each** *soldier* has a gun in his hand.
    (b) **Each** *guest* was given an ice-cream.

WHO, WHOM, WHOSE, WHICH, WHAT

These pronouns can be used both as **interrogative** and **relative** *pronouns.*

(a) WHO, WHOM, WHOSE always refer to people ; as—
   1. **Who** is there at the door ?
   2. **Whom** do you want to see ?   — *as interrogative pronouns*
   3. **Whose** is this beautiful pen ?

(b) 1. He is the boy **who** stole my pen.
     2. She is the girl **whom** I shall marry.   — *as relative pronouns*
     3. Let me know **whose** pen is this.

B. WHAT, WHICH

(a) 1. **What** are you doing here ?
     2. **Which** came first, the egg or the chicken ?   — *as interrogative pronouns*

(b) 3. Let me know **what** you want.
     4. This is the house in **which** I was born.   — *as relative pronouns*

C. THAT

It can refer to both *people* and to *objects*. It is used as a *relative pronoun* ; as—
   1. She is the girl **that** I shall wed.
   2. Which is the bed **that** I am to sleep in ?

OTHER PRONOUNS

Many other words can also be used as *pronouns*. These words are :

all	both	few	many	much
neither	either	any	enough	most
some	several	more	little	

All the words given above are determiners also. The only way to know what each of them is—a *pronoun* or a *determiner*—is as under :

1. If any of these words stands alone for a noun, it is a pronoun.
2. But if it is followed by a noun, it is a determiner.

TEST YOURSELF

A. Given below are sentences in which *you, we, they* are used to give a general meaning—*people* or *mankind*. Complete each sentence :

1. You cannot .... everybody.
2. We must .... what we cannot cure.
3. We are like actors and the world is like a ....
4. They say that virtue is ....
5. This is what ....call true love.
6. ....never die who die for a great cause.
7. .... cannot serve two masters at a time.
8. .... cannot live without air, water and food.
9. .... can make your career through your deeds.
10. ....are going to ban the practice of slavery.

B. Write two sentences using—*it*—to refer to :

(a) time :
   1. ....
   2. ....

(b) day :
   1. ....
   2. ....

(c) date :
   1. ....
   2. ....

(d) weather :
   1. ....
   2. ....

(e) situations :
1. ....
2. ....

(f) an impersonal subject :
1. ....
2. ....

(g) an object to a verb :
1. ....
2. ....

(h) a person :
1. ....
2. ....

(i) cost :
1. ....
2. ....

(j) duration :
1. ....
2. ....

(k) with the verb—need :
1. ....
2. ....

(l) to express comments :
1. ....
2. ....

C. **Write whether the word in bold type is a *pronoun* or a *determiner* :**

1. This idea is **mine,** not of anybody else. ....
2. This is **his** car. ....
3. This car is **his.** ....
4. **Each** player has a bat in his hand. ....
5. **This** was not fair on your part. ....

6. Do you like **this** shirt or that ? ....
7. **Little** can be done to help them. ....
8. **Most** people are innocent, I think. ....
9. **Either** side of the road has shady trees. ....
10. **Either** of the two sisters is tall and slim. ....
11. **Enough** has been said on this point. ....
12. One girl was whispering to **another**. ....
13. **Which** came first—the chicken or the egg ? ....
14. **What** have you come here for ? ....
15. He is the man **who** has won an award. ....
16. **Whose** is this lovable baby ? ....

D. Each sentence has a *reflexive pronoun*. Which of them has been used *as an object* and which *for emphasis* :

1. History repeats **itself**, they say. ....
2. All of us introduced **ourselves** to one another. ....
3. Go and buy a new shirt for **yourself**. ....
4. I **myself** shall meet her and settle the dispute. ....
5. The queen looked at **herself** in the mirror. ....
6. We **ourselves** should build up our strength. ....
7. My uncle lives in New York **itself**. ....
8. He **himself** can achieve much more. ....
9. She rushed out slamming the door behind **herself**. ....
10. None of us can cook for **himself** or **herself**. ....

E. Define—

(a) a *reflexive pronoun*. Give an example also.
....
Example : ....

(b) an *emphasizing reflexive pronoun*. Give an example also.
....
Example : ....

5 ADJECTIVES : IMPORTANT FACTS

We have studied nouns, pronouns and determiners in the previous chapters. In this chapter, we shall study important facts about **adjectives**.

WHAT ARE ADJECTIVES ?

Adjectives *describe nouns (things, places and people) giving various types of information about them.*

We must know the following facts about adjectives :

1. Where is the subject placed—**before its noun** or **after the verb** ?
2. What **type** of adjective is it ?
3. Does the **form** of an adjective ever change ?
4. Are **number** and **quantity** words—*adjectives* or *determiners* ?

PLACEMENT OF AN ADJECTIVE

When an adjective is to express a noun in an ordinary manner, it is placed before its noun ; as—

hot *coffee*   **chilly** *weather*   **polite** *talk*

When an adjective is to express a noun **focussing attention** on its adjective, the adjective is placed after the verb ; as—

1. Her *smile* is **bewitching.**
2. The *earthquake* was very **severe.**
3. At my words, he became **angry.**
4. The *point* is quite **clear** now.
5. The *evening* was **cool** and **pleasant.**

ADJECTIVES AND DETERMINERS

We know that determiners are words that were formerly included in adjectives. But now they form a different part of speech. They include—

1. Number Words   2. Quantity Words   3. Articles
4. Possessives   5. Demonstratives   6. Post Determiners

TYPES OF ADJECTIVES

Adjectives have the following eight types :

1. Adjectives of Quality   2. Adjectives of Colour

3. Adjectives of Class
4. Emphasizing Adjectives
5. Participle Adjectives
6. Proper Adjectives
7. Interrogative Adjectives
8. Compound Adjectives

1. ADJECTIVES OF QUALITY

An *adjective of quality* is an adjective that identifies a quality that its noun has ; as—

a **sad** *tale*   a **charming** *lady*   a **little** *child*
a **wealthy** *person*   a **wise** *man*   a **happy** *mother*

2. ADJECTIVES OF COLOUR

An *adjective of colour* is an adjective that identifies a colour of the noun described by it ; as—

blue *eyes*   a **red** *apple*   **yellow** *ribbons*
a **light brown** *dress*   a **black** *cat*   a **greenish** *glass*

3. ADJECTIVES OF CLASS

An *adjective of class* is an adjective that identifies a particular class which its noun belongs to ; as—

the **central** *idea*   **financial** *help*   a **cultural** *programme*
domestic *animals*   **religious** *books*   a **political** *party*

4. EMPHASIZING ADJECTIVES

An *emphasizing adjective* is an adjective that lays stress on some feeling or quality of its noun ; as—

an **urgent** *need*   in **utter** *despair*   a **pure** *love*
a **thorough** *gentleman*   **total** *failure*   a **complete** *idiot*
to the **very** *end*

5. PARTICIPLE ADJECTIVES

A *participle adjective* is an adjective that is, in fact, a participle but is used as an adjective ; as—

Participle Adjectives are of two types :

(a) ing-adjectives   (b) ed-adjectives

Examples :

(a) **ing-adjectives** are, in fact, *present participles* ; as—

| an **interesting** *story* | a **charming** *scenery* | an **exciting** *idea* |
| a **pleasing** *personality* | an **alarming** *increase* | a **boring** *lecture* |

(b) **ed-adjectives** are, in fact, *past participles* ; as—

| a **tired** *traveller* | a **broken** *heart* | a **satisfied** *person* |
| an **agitated** *crowd* | **frightened** *animals* | a **furnished** *flat* |

6. PROPER ADJECTIVES

A *proper adjective* is an adjective that is formed from a *proper noun* ; as—

American *citizens*	the **Swiss** *Chocolates*	a **Herculean** *task*
Victorian *Age*	the **French** *cut*	the **English** *Channel*
Napoleonic *Wars*	**Shakespearean** *play*	**British** *ladies*

7. INTERROGATIVE ADJECTIVES

An *interrogative adjective* is an adjective that is used to ask a question regarding the noun that follows it ; as—

1. **Which** *book* is this ?
2. **Which** *pen* do you like best ?

8. COMPOUND ADJECTIVES

A *compound adjective* is an adjective that is made up of two or more words usually with hyphens between them ; as—

a **bottle-green** *car*	a **low-paid** *job*	**one-way** *traffic*
an **air-conditioned** *room*	a **good-looking** *girl*	a **five-rupee** *note*
an **up-to-date** *account*	a **to-the-point** *argument*	a **do-or-die** *effort*

USE OF ADJECTIVES

Remember the following facts about the use of adjectives :

A. ATTRIBUTIVE USE

One way of using adjectives is to place them before their nouns. In this form, the adjective only gives some information about the noun. In other words, its importance is less than its noun ; as—

a *wonderful* **picture**   a *fascinating* **smile**   a *technical* **term**

This use of the adjectives is called their **attributive use**.

B. PREDICATIVE USE

The other way of using adjectives is to place them after the verbs as **complements**. In this use, the adjective catches the attention of the reader and becomes *more important* than its noun ; as—

The *man* is **dead**.   He was **angry**.
The *evening* was **pleasant**.   The *food* was **tasty**.

This use of adjectives is called their **predicative use**.

ADJECTIVES FOR COMPARISONS

Adjectives are describing words. Most of them describe the qualities of nouns. So, they are *gradable words*. It means that the quality denoted by the adjective can be more or less in one noun than in another noun. For this purpose, adjectives are used in three different forms.

Stating the degrees of a quality in two different nouns is called their *comparison.*

Comparisons can express three types of facts :

(a) Two nouns may possess a quality of the same degree.

(b) One noun may possess a quality to a higher or lower degree than another noun.

(c) One noun may possess a quality to the highest degree—higher than all other nouns.

So, most adjectives have three different forms to be used in different types of comparison. Let us study them.

A. POSITIVE FORM

This is the *usual form* **of an adjective ;** as—

good   bad   quiet   tall   charming

This usual form is used in two ways :

(a) **To simply describe the quality of a noun** (*no comparison*)

1. Erika was a **charming** queen.
2. The Taj is a very **grand** building.

(b) **To state that two nouns have or don't have a quality to the same degree :**

1. Mary is *as* **tall** *as* Erika.   (*Positive*)
2. Mary is not *so* **tall** *as* Erika.   (*Negative*)

B. COMPARATIVE FORM

This form of an adjective is used to state that a noun has a quality to a higher or lower degree than another noun :

1. This stone is **heavier** than that.
2. Dory is **less intelligent** than Erika.
3. Stone is **harder than** cotton.
4. The **higher** we go, the **cooler** it is.

The comparative form is formed in two ways :

1. *By adding* **er** *to the usual form of the adjective :*

   large → **larger** quiet → **quieter** slim → **slimmer**

2. *By using the word*—**more**—*before the usual form of the adjective :*

   intelligent → **more intelligent** interesting → **more interesting**

☞ *We use the word*—**than**—*after the comparative form of an adjective.*

SUPERLATIVE FORM

This form of an adjective is used to state that a noun possesses a quality to the highest degree :

1. Mac is *the* **tallest** boy in the class.
2. The Himalayas are *the* **highest** mountains in the world.
3. Terrorism is *the* **worst** danger for mankind.

Or

1. Mac is *the* **tallest** *of* all the boys.
2. The Himalayas are *the* **highest** *of* all the mountains.
3. Terrorism is *the* **worst** *of* all the dangers.

Note the following facts carefully :

1. The superlative form of an adjective is preceded by **the.**
2. It is followed by **of** or **in.**
3. The superlative forms of adjectives are formed in two different ways :

   (a) *By adding* **est** *to the usual form* of the adjective ; as—

   tall → **tallest** bright → **brightest** hard → **hardest**

(b) By using **most** before the usual form ; as—

most **intelligent**   most **dangerous**   most **interesting**

4. The word **most** does not always stand for the superlative form of the adjective that follows it. When it is not used for a comparison, it does not take *the* before it and it means *very, very*.
   1. It is **most unfortunate** indeed.
   2. It is a **most interesting** story.
   3. She is a **most extraordinary** lady.

TEST YOURSELF

A. Answer the following questions :

1. What job do *adjectives* do ?
   ....
   ....

2. Where is an *adjective placed* in a sentence ?
   ....
   ....

3. What are *attributive adjectives* ? Give three examples.
   ....
   Examples : ....

4. What are *predicative adjectives* ? Give three examples :
   Examples : ....

5. How many *kinds* of adjectives are there ? Name them.
   ....
   ....
   ....
   ....

6. How many *forms* do most adjectives have ? Name them.
   ....
   ....

B. Given below are ten sentences, each with an *adjective*. Underline it and write in the blank whether its use is *attributive* or *predicative* :

1. A *lame* horse is grazing in the field. ....
2. The lass is really *charming*. ....
3. James is a *brilliant* student. ....
4. The king's palace is very *magnificent*. ....
5. Your uncle is a *noble* person. ....
6. That point is quite *clear* now. ....
7. This is a *novel* idea indeed. ....
8. We have a *clear cut* plan for today. ....
9. This amount is *sufficient* for this project. ....

C. Given below are fifteen sentences, each with an *adjective*. Underline each adjective and name its *kind* :

1. Our annual test will start tomorrow. ....
2. The English Alphabet has 26 letters. ....
3. Here is a five-dollar bill for you. ....
4. Her eyes are so sparkling. ....
5. The rotten apples were thrown away. ....
6. Our country has many political parties. ....
7. She is wearing a pale green frock. ....
8. My father is fond of western music. ....
9. What colour are your shoes ? ....
10. An empty vessel makes much noise. ....
11. He was my class-mate at school. ....
12. Honest persons are respected everywhere. ....
13. Ladies are singing songs on the roof. ....
14. Church bell chimes as early as 6-00 a.m. ....

D. Each sentence has an *adjective* used in it. Underline it and name its *form* in the blank :

1. Dogs and horses are faithful animals. ....

2. You are even more cunning than a fox. ....
3. She is the prettiest of all the three sisters. ....
4. He is a man of few words. ....
5. Spring is the best of all the seasons of the year. ....
6. The elephant is the biggest land animal. ....
7. Men are far tougher than women. ....
8. This sum is quite easy. ....

INTERCHANGE OF ADJECTIVE FORMS

We can transform sentences with different forms of adjectives used in them. Let us study how to do it.

A. POSITIVE TO COMPARATIVE

Observe the following examples :

1. Mac is as hardworking as Alfred. *(positive)*
   Mac is *not less hardworking* than Alfred. *(comparative)*

2. Erika is *not so tall* as Lucy. *(positive)*
   Erika is *less tall* than Lucy. *(comparative)*

B. COMPARATIVE TO POSITIVE

Observe the following examples :

1. This boy is *cleverer* than that boy. *(comparative)*
   That boy is *not so clever* as this boy. *(positive)*
2. Neither boy is *cleverer* than the other. *(comparative)*
   Both the boys are equally *clever*. *(positive)*.

C. POSITIVE TO SUPERLATIVE

Observe the following examples :

1. No other boy is *so tall* as James. *(positive)*
   James is the *tallest* of all the boys. *(superlative)*
2. No other peak is *so high* as Mount Everest. *(positive)*
   Mount Everest is the *highest* peak. *(superlative)*

D. SUPERLATIVE TO POSITIVE

Observe the following examples :

1. James is my *closest* friend. *(superlative)*
   No other friend of mine is *so close* to me as James. *(positive)*
2. Pumpkin is the *cheapest* vegetable. *(superlative)*
   No other vegetable is *so cheap* as pumpkin. *(positive)*

E. COMPARATIVE TO SUPERLATIVE

Observe the following examples :

1. No other city in France is *larger* than Paris. *(comparative)*
   Paris is the *largest* city in France. *(superlative)*
2. Most other cities in France are *smaller* than Paris. *(comparative)*
   Paris is one of the *largest* cities in France. *(superlative)*

F. SUPERLATIVE TO COMPARATIVE

1. Bill Gates is the *richest* person in the US. *(superlative)*
   No other person is *richer* than Bill Gates in the US. *(comparative)*
2. Bill Gates is one of the *richest* person in the US. *(superlative)*
   Most other persons in the US are *less rich* than Bill Gates. *(comparative)*

TEST YOURSELF

Do as directed :

1. This tree is as tall as that. (Rewrite using comparative form)
   (a) ....
   (b) ....
2. The Eiffel Tower is the largest structure in France.
   (Rewrite using positive and comparative forms)
   (a) ....
   (b) ....
3. Few animals are as useful as the camel.
   (Rewrite using comparative and superlative forms)
   (a) ....
   (b) ....

4. This development is most unfortunate. *(Rewrite using positive form and comparative form)*
   (a) ....
   (b) ....

MORE ABOUT ADJECTIVE FORMS

A. When we use the *comparative form* of an adjective for selection out of two nouns, we use *the* before it and it is followed by *of* ; as—

1. James is **the** *taller* **of** the two brothers.
2. Which **of** the two books is **the** *better* one ?

B. Four foreign adjectives—*junior, senior, inferior, superior*—are followed by *to* not by *than* ; as—

1. He is *senior* **to** me in age
2. I am *junior* **to** him in service.
3. This pen is *superior* **to** that.
4. That chair is *inferior* **to** this.

C. *Double comparatives* are incorrect ; as—

1. A fox is **more cleverer** than a jackal.   *(incorrect)*
   A fox is *far* **cleverer** than a jackal.   *(correct)*
2. This baby is **more lovelier** than that.   *(incorrect)*
   This baby is *much* **lovelier** than that.   *(correct)*

D. When we use a *superlative degree* after a *possessive word*, *the* is not used ; as—

   my *best* friend   **his** *most favourite* game   **her** *worst nightmare*

E. When *no comparison* is meant, but only *a very high degree* is to be stated, the superlative degree does not take *the* before it ; as—

1. It was **most unwise** on your part.
2. We will be **worst hit** by this law.

F. *Double superlatives* are also incorrect ; as—

1. Steve is the **most wealthiest** Japanese trader.   *(incorrect)*
2. Japan is the **most largest** market for selling goods.   *(incorrect)*

   The correct forms are—

1. Steve is **by far the wealthiest** Japanese trader.
2. Japan is **by far the largest** market for selling goods.

TEST YOURSELF

A. Change each sentence *as directed* :

1. He is as silly as an ass.

    (use comparative form)

    ....

2. The air on hills is cooler than that in plains.

    (use positive form)

    ....

3. Antwerp is the best sea-port in Europe.

    (use positive and comparative forms)

    (a) ....

    (b) ....

4. King George V was one of the greatest emperors of Britain.

    (use positive and comparative form)

    (a) ....

    (b) ....

5. Few metals are as costly as gold.

    (use comparative form)

    ....

6. It is easier to say than to do a thing.

    (use positive form)

    ....

7. Bad health is a more dangerous enemy than poverty.

    (use positive form)

    ....

8. The elder brother is not so clever as the younger.
    (use comparative form)

    ....

9. Platinum is as heavy as gold.

    (use comparative form)

    ....

44

B. Correct each sentence :

1. Which is the tallest of the two brothers ?
   ....

2. Milk is a superior food than most foods.
   ....

3. She is the oldest of the three sisters.
   ....

4. A fox is more clever than a jackal.
   ....

5. Which is the elder, you or him ?
   ....

6. Water is more commoner a liquid than any other liquid.
   ....

C. Explain the difference :

1. (a) I love you more than he.
   (b) I love you more than him.
   (a) ....
   (b) ....

2. (a) The older boy is slimmer also.
   (b) The elder brother is a famous doctor.
   (a) ....
   (b) ....

3. (a) He is senior to me in age.
   (b) He is senior to me in service.
   (a) ....
   (b) ....

4. (a) This is a tiring job.
   (b) I am tired of this job.
   (a) ....
   (b) ....

6. ADVERBS: IMPORTANT FACTS

WHAT ARE ADVERBS ?

Adverbs are used to add to the meaning of any part of speech except a noun or pronoun.

Observe the following examples :

1. The lion *roared* **loudly**.   *(qualifying a verb)*
2. The lion roared **very** *loudly*.   *(qualifying an adverb)*
3. An ass is an **extremely** *silly* animal.   *(qualifying an adjective)*
4. The village is **almost** *on* the edge of the forest. *(qualifying a preposition)*
5. I shall come **only** *when* you are there.   *(qualifying a conjunction)*

TYPES OF ADVERBS

Adverbs fall into three classes :

(a) Simple Adverbs   (b) Interrogative Adverbs   (c) Relative Adverbs

SIMPLE ADVERBS

Simple Adverbs can be classified into the following kinds :

A. ADVERBS OF TIME

1. He reached here **yesterday**.
2. He had done it **before** I reached.

Commonly used *adverbs of time* are :

now	then	before	since	ago
already	presently	early	late	today
afterwards	immediately	tomorrow	yesterday	soon

B. ADVERBS OF PLACE

1. Please come **here**.
2. Who is **there** at the door ?

Commonly used *adverbs of place* are :

| here | there | hither | thither | in |

46

out	within	without	above	below
inside	outside	near	far	hence

C. ADVERBS OF MANNER

1. The tortoise moved **slowly** but **steadily**.
2. Always do your work **carefully**.

Commonly used *adverbs of manner* are :

thus	so	well	ill	badly
carefully	certainly	similarly	probably	surely

D. ADVERBS OF EXTENT/DEGREE

1. He is **almost** on the verge of death   *(extent)*
2. Your work is **quite** OK.   *(degree)*
3. It looks **somewhat** awkward.   *(degree)*
4. **The** higher we go, **the** cooler it is.   *(extent)*

E. ADVERBS OF AFFIRMATION AND NEGATION

1. **Yes**, he came to see me.   2. **No**, he never came here.

These verbs include—

yes	no	not
not at all	by all means	by no means

F. ADVERBS OF FREQUENCY

1. I did it **once** by mistake.
2. I will not repeat this mistake **again**.
3. Two of a trade **seldom** agree.
4. He **often** comes to see me.

These adverbs include—

once	twice	thrice	again	seldom	often
never	always	sometimes	firstly	secondly	thirdly

INTERROGATIVE ADVERBS

Interrogative adverbs are used to ask questions. They fall into as many kinds as the simple adverbs :

A. TIME
1. **When** do you get up ?
2. **How long** will you be here ?

B. PLACE
1. **Where** do you live ?
2. **Where** is your mind wandering ?

C. FREQUENCY
1. **How often** do you take tea every day ?

D. MANNER
1. **How** did you solve this sum ?
2. **How** are you, Michael ?

E. DEGREE/EXTENT
How far is his claim justified ?

F. REASON
Why have you come so late ?

RELATIVE ADVERBS

All the *interrogative adverbs* are used as **relative adverbs**. Instead of asking questions, they do the job of joining two sentences. Given below are examples of various types of relative adverbs :

A. TIME
1. Her father died **when** she was quite young.
2. Your father wants to see him **before** he dies.

B. PLACE
1. He is happy **where** he is.
2. **Wherever** I went, I was welcomed warmly.

C. MANNER
1. Let him behave **as** he does.
2. He talks **as if** he were mad.

D. PURPOSE
1. Walk carefully **lest** you should fall.
2. I bought a cow **so that** I might have milk to drink.

E. REASON
1. Ask her why she has come late.

F. EXTENT
1. Let me know **how much** money you want.
2. Explain to me **how far** you have been successful.

COMPARISON OF ADVERBS

Some adverbs have their forms to be used for comparison just as adjectives have. These forms are formed in the following three ways :

A. By adding *er* and *est* :

Positive	Comparative	Superlative
soon	sooner	soonest
long	longer	longest
loud	louder	loudest
late	later	latest/last
near	nearer	nearest
early	earlier	earliest

B. By adding *ly* :

wisely	more wisely	most wisely
beautifully	more beautifully	most beautifully
carefully	more carefully	most carefully

C. Irregular forms :

well	better	best
ill/badly	worse	worst
much	more	most
little	less	least
forth	further	furthest
far	farther	farthest
near	nearer	nearest

SOME ADVERBIAL PHRASES

1. **at random** = *haphazard ; unplanned*
   The data was collected *at random* to begin with.

2. **of course** = *undoubtedly*
   Of course, she is the best of all the models.

3. **at length** = *finally*
   At length, the rebels laid down their arms.

4. **in fact** = *actually*
   This is, *in fact*, a typing error.

5. **in general** = *generally*
   People, *in general*, are God-fearing and kind.

6. **in particular** = *specially*
   His name was included in the list *in particular*.

7. **in short** = *briefly*
   In short, we must be exact in calculations.

8. **in vain** = *useless*
   The fox tried hard to get at the grapes but all *in vain*.

9. **after all** = *whatever be said against*
   Children are *after all* children.

10. **at first** = *first of all*
    We must finish this job *at first*.

11. **at least** = *in the minimum*
    You must be respectful to elders *at least*.

12. **at most** = *the maximum*
    What can he do *at most* ?

13. **at all** = *in no way/degree*
    I will not betray my country *at all*.

14. **at present** = *at this time*
    What is the condition of your business *at present* ?

15. **for ever** = *for all time*
    He has left America *for ever* to settle in London.

16. **at once** = *immediately*
   Run away from this place *at once*.

17. **by all means** = *certainly*
   By all means you can have another cup of tea.

18. **by no means** = *not at all*
   By no means I can believe that we are following the right path.

19. **by the way** = **by the by** = *incidently*
   By the way I bumped into a policeman.

20. **by and large** = *on the whole*
   By and large he is an efficient cook.

21. **by and by** = *in due course ; before long*
   By and by he will come to the right path.

22. **up and down** = *backwards and forwards*
   The sentry is walking *up and down* before the gate.

23. **to and fro** = *back and forth*
   The visitor is pacing *to and fro* in the verandah.

24. **here and there** = *hither and thither*
   The thirsty crow flew *here and there* for water.

25. **now and then** = *occasionally*
   He comes to see me every *now and then*.

26. **off and on** = *irregularly*
   It has been raining *off and on* since morning.

27. **now or never** = *either now or never*
   You won't have a second chance ; it is *now or never*.

28. **on and on** = *in continuing action*
   This boring lecture seems to go *on and on*.

29. **inside out** = *reversed*
   You have put on your shirt *inside out*.

30. **upside down** = *turned over*
   Hold the bag *upside down* to shake out the last crumbs.

31. **above all** = *before anything else*
   Above all we must say our prayers to the Lord.

32. **above board** = *open ; non-secret*
    1. I always do things *above board*.
    2. His honesty is quite *above board*.
33. **as it were** = *If I'm allowed to say so*
    A teacher is, *as it were*, the mental father of his/her pupils.
34. **as yet** = *till now (refers to past time)*
    I have never failed a test *as yet*.
35. **before long** = *in a short time*
    He must return safe and sound *before long*.
36. **far and away** = *out and out* = *decidedly*
    This candidate is *far and away (out and out)* the best of the lot.
37. **far and near** = *from all directions*
    People come to see the show from *far and near*.
38. **far and wide** = *to all directions*
    His fame as a painter has spread *far and wide*.
39. **first and foremost** = *the very first*
    Our *first and foremost* duty is to work honestly.
40. **in time** = *(i) by the proper time ; (ii) eventually, in due course*
    1. We could not get there *in time*.
    2. We must help one another in times of need.
41. **in the long run** = *eventually*
    A cheat gets exposed *in the long run*.
42. **on the contrary** = *far from*
    I don't like that man ; *on the contrary*, I hate him.
43. **to the contrary** = *against*
    I have nothing to say *to the contrary* of what you have said.
44. **once for all** = *never to be taken up again*
    Settle your dispute *once for all*.
45. **over and above** = *additionally*
    I was injured and insulted *over and above*.
46. **through and through** = *completely*
    We were drenched *through and through* in the heavy rain.

47. **what not** = *many more*

    The trade fair deals with sales promotion, product branding and what not.

48. **on the alert** = *watchful*

    Always be *on the alert* for anything suspicious.

49. **out of** = *due to*

    This was all done by her *out of* jealousy.

50. **greatly to** = *it goes to*

    Greatly to his credit, he stood first.

51. **close to** = *very near*

    A theatre is close to the grocery shop.

52. **close on/upon** = *almost touching*

    The lamb followed Mary close *upon* her heels.

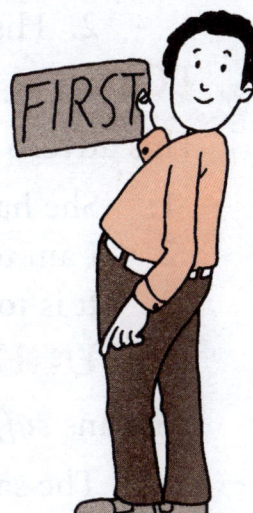

USE OF ADVERBS

Just like adjectives, adverbs are also used in two ways :

(a) When an adverb qualifies its word in an ordinary way remaining *less important* than its word, its use is **attributive** ; as—

1. You are **totally** wrong.
2. The building is **badly** damaged.
3. The young boy is **utterly** innocent.

(b) When an adverb is used as a complement, *i.e.* as a part of the predicate, it is *more important* than its word and its use is **predicative** ; as—

1. He will be **better** before long.
2. The bear was caught **alive**.
3. We are **aware** of our shortcomings.

SOME SPECIAL ADVERBS

A. MUCH, VERY

(a) **Much** qualifies adjectives in the *comparative degree* and also *past participles* ; as—

1. The weather is **much** *hotter* today than it was yesterday.
2. I was **much** *surprised* to hear her words.

53

(b) **Very** is used as an *emphasizing adjective* and also to *qualify adverbs*; as—

1. He is the **very** same *man* who beat me yesterday.
2. His performance is **very** *much better*.

B. TOO

This adverb indicates *excess, i.e. more than enough* ; as—

1. She has been **too** *good* indeed.
2. I am **too** *happy* to see you here.
3. It is **too** *hot* to go out.

C. ENOUGH

It means *sufficient, i.e.* it denotes the *proper limit* ; as—

1. The salary is *high* **enough** for the job.
2. The patient is *strong* **enough** to move about.

D. SINCE

This word is used as an *adverb of time*. It has three different meanings :

(a) *From that time* ; as—

1. I saw her two years ago and have remembered her **since**.
2. He has been down with fever **since** yesterday.

(b) *At some time between then and now* ; as—

1. He met me last week and has rung me up several times **since then**.
2. I was at school with him but have seen him only twice **since**.

(c) *From now (backwards)*

1. That was very long **since** indeed.

E. AGO

It is used as an *adverb* in the phrase long *ago* ; as—

1. It happened to me *long* **ago**.

F. BEFORE

As an adverb, it means *on a former occasion* ; as—

1. I did so *once* **before** but I will do it again now.
2. Never **before** did I see such a horrible sight.

G. ALREADY

It means *prior to the time mentioned* ; as—
1. I have **already** lighted the gas stove.
2. She has **already** completed her 20th year.

H. AGAIN

(a) It means *a second time* ; as—
1. I warn you not to come here **again**.
2. You have not done it properly ; do it **again**.

(b) *The same thing repeated* ; as—
1. The rate fell back **again** to its original level.
2. You have made enough mistakes, so don't repeat it again.

(c) *Moreover* ; as—

Again, it is now too late ; so it is no use going there.

I. INDEED

It has three senses as under :

(a) *Certainly* ; as—
1. That was **indeed** a big blunder on our part.
2. It is **indeed** a very difficult job.

(b) *Truly speaking (used as an interjection)* ; as—
1. **Indeed !** I cannot help you in this matter.
2. **Indeed !** you are not capable of doing this.

(c) *It is admitted, but* ; as—
1. I may be good at studies **indeed,** but not in sports.
2. It is true in words **indeed,** not in practice.

TEST YOURSELF

A. Answer the following questions :

1. What are *adverbs* ?

....

....

2. How many *kinds* of adverbs are there ? Name them.
   ....
   ....
3. Name the six types of simple adverbs :
   ....
   ....
   ....

B. Write the two other forms of the following *adverbs* :
   1. well   ....
   2. ill   ....
   3. forth   ....
   4. far   ....

C. Use each of the following *phrases* into a sentence :
   1. at length   : ....
   2. in vain   : ....
   3. at all   : ....
   4. at once   : ....
   5. off and on   : ....
   6. inside out   : ....
   7. on and on   : ....
   8. out and out   : ....
   9. far and near   : ....
   10. far and wide   : ....

D. Give two examples of the *attributive use* of adverbs and two of their predicative use :
   (a) 1. ....
       2. ....
   (b) 1. ....
       2. ....

E. Fill up each sentence with a *suitable adverb* :
   1. The weather is .... hotter today than it was yesterday.
   2. She is .... woman who was arrested for shop-lifting.

2. He.. invited me to visit him.
3. It is not good to be .... good indeed.
4. Our army is strong .... to defeat the enemy.
5. We met in 1998. We have written to each other ....
6. .... did I see such a charming scenery.
7. One number is half as much ....as the other.
8. ....! I have no money to start a business.
9. This is .... a big blunder on your part, Alfred.
10. Our business is strong .... to go ahead smoothly.
11. My father is laid up with fever .... January 2008.
12. Your answer is incorrect. Do the sum once ....
13. This time, his performance is ....better.
14. The young boy is wise .... for his years.
15. James is clever .... to see through his tricks.

F. **Given below are fifteen sentences each with an *adverb*. Underline the *adverb* and write its *kind* and *type* in the blank :**

1. He is almost on the verge of starvation. ....
2. How did you get to the hill top ? ....
3. Her mother died when she was just a child. ....
4. How far have you to go still ? ....
5. He reached here from Europe yesterday. ....
6. Walk carefully lest you should stumble. ....
7. My son has already completed his 9th year. ....
8. Incident took place long ago. ....
9. We have lived in this house since 1992. ....
10. Never before did I see such a beauty. ....
11. The donkey is an extremely silly animal. ....
12. The tortoise moved slowly towards its goal. ....
13. Your words seem somewhat strange to me. ....
14. How far is she justified in doing so ? ....
15. My uncle wants to see you before he leaves. ....

7. PREPOSITIONS : IMPORTANT FACTS

A preposition is a *small word that denotes the relation between two nouns/pronouns used in the same sentence.*

Different prepositions denote different relations. Let us study some of them.

A. ABOUT : shows *nearness of time, place, state, etc.* ; as—

1. He must be somewhere **about**. (place)
2. It is **about** seven o'clock. (time)
3. She enquired **about** your health. (state)
4. Go **about** your business honestly. (occupation)

B. ABOVE : *higher than* over

1. A sword hung **above** my head.
2. My expenditure is **above** my income.
3. He is **above** such meanness.

C. ACROSS : *crossing from one side to another*

1. We all swam **across** the river.
2. The beam fell **across** the street.
3. Lay the bundle **across** your shoulder.

D. AFTER: shows *sequence in place, time, effect, similarity etc.;* as—

1. I will leave this place **after** you. (place)
2. He arrived here **after** nightfall. (time)
3. I have said this **after** reading both the statements. (effect)
4. The boy takes **after** his father. (similarity)

E. AGAINST : shows *opposition*

1. The old man leaned **against** the wall. (place)
2. You are acting **against** your own family. (relation)
3. Keep on the alert **against** idleness. (opposition)
4. Four votes are **against** the move. (proportion)

F. ALONG : *in line with*

1. We trudged along the dusty high way. (place)
2. I have a walk along the river-side every day. (place)

G. At : shows *closeness to time, place, state, effect, value, aim, occupation* ; as—

   1. **At** what price can we buy the microwave ? *(place)*
   2. We reached here yesterday **at** 4 o'clock. *(time)*
   3. He is feeling quite **at** ease now. *(state)*
   4. He felt annoyed **at** my words. *(effect)*
   5. **At** what rate is sugar sold ? *(value)*
   6. Children are **at** play in the park. *(action)*

H. BEFORE : *opposite of* **behind**

   1. The sentry stood **before** the gate. *(place)*
   2. The train reached **before** time. *(time)*
   3. Death **before** dishonour. *(choice)*

I. BEHIND : *at the back*

   1. A tree stood **behind** the hut. *(place)*
   2. The train is running **behind** time. *(time)*
   3. There is a storm **behind** this calm. *(happening)*

J. BY : shows *nearness, manner, means*

   1. Come inside and sit **by** me, dear. *(place)*
   2. Birds reach their nests **by** sunset. *(time)*
   3. I was duly entertained **by** him. *(means)*
   4. I caught him **by** the arm. *(manner)*
   5. He swore **by** his son. *(adjuration)*
   6. He is cleverer than I **by** a good deal. *(measure)*

K. FOR : *in place of ; for the sake of*

   1. They will leave **for** home soon. *(place)*
   2. He has been imprisoned **for** life. *(time)*
   3. **For** what has he been arrested ? *(cause)*
   4. **For** all his learning, he has no common sense. *(presence)*
   5. He sold his house **for** a small amount. *(value)*
   6. He did a lot **for** all of us. *(sake)*
   7. It is a *word* **for** *word* translation. *(exchange)*
   8. He is not fit **for** this job. *(ability)*

L.   FROM : *used for separation from anything*

1. He is away **from** home.   (place)
2. We all work **from** Monday to Saturday.   (time)
3. He has descended **from** noble fore-fathers.   (source)
4. **From** all these facts, he looks to be mad.   (result)
5. Idleness breeds **from** laziness.   (motive)
6. It is easy to know a fool **from** a wise man.   (distinction)

M.   IN : *inside a thing*

1. He is **in** the house now.   (place)
2. I will return **in** a week.   (time)
3. He is **in** a bad temper at this time.   (manner)
4. I've found a true friend **in** him.   (reference)

N.   INTO : *motion towards the inside of a thing*

1. I kept studying till late **into** the night.   (time)
2. A stream flows **into** another.   (place)
3. Water changes **into** steam on heating.   (state)
4. Pour tea **into** four cups.   (motion)

O.   OF : *belonging to ; coming from*

1. What did he die **of** ?   (cause)
2. He comes **of** a noble family.   (relation)
3. He was deprived **of** his property.   (separation)
4. He is a man **of** steel.   (quality)
5. He sent me a packet **of** sweets.   (contents)
6. This box is made **of** leather.   (material)
7. He lived in the house **of** his uncle.   (belonging)
8. What are you thinking **of** ?   (relation)
9. The horse is lame **of** one leg.   (reference)

P. TO : *towards*

1. She returned **to** her father's house.   (place)
2. He has reached here just **to**-day.   (time)
3. **To** all appearances, he is tired.   (possibility)
4. The chances are three **to** one.   (ratio)
5. They fought **to** the last man.   (limit)
6. **To** my dismay, he failed the test.   (effect)
7. He is coming **to** dine with us.   (purpose)

Q. **WITH** : *attachment*

1. She arrived **with** all her luggage. (place)
2. Frogs start croaking **with** the rainfall. (time)
3. I do not agree **with** him at all. (agreement)
4. The enemies fought **with** each other. (opposition)
5. I will never part **with** this book. (separation)
6. He is popular **with** his students. (attachment)
7. **With** all his wealth, he lives like a beggar. (despite)
8. He killed the snake **with** a stone. (instrument)
9. He looked at me **with** anger. (manner)
10. She is laid up **with** fever. (cause)

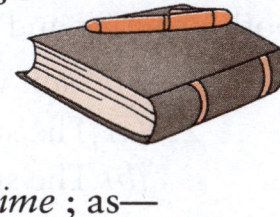

KNOW THE DIFFERENCE

at, in

At denotes a *small distance* but **in** denotes a *wider one* ; as—

1. He was at his wits end since he could not solve the problem.
2. The job **in** hand will take time.

with, by

With is related to the *instrument* but **by** to the *doer* ; as—

1. The book was written **with** a pen.
2. The book was written **by** Martin.

in, after

After is related to the *passed time* but **in** to the *future time* ; as—

1. The patient died **after** a prolonged illness.
2. I shall return **in** about a week.

between, among

Between is used for *two nouns* while **among** for *more than two* ; as—

1. The two brothers quarrelled **between** themselves.
2. All the ministers divided the money **among** themselves.

beside, besides

beside = *by the side of* ; **besides** = *in addition to*

1. My brother came and sat **beside** me.
2. **Besides** advising, he helped me with money also.

by, before, since

All the three are used for a **point of time**, not for a *period of time* ; as—

1. I must be back **by** 5:00 p.m.
2. He will not leave **before** 5:00 p.m.
3. It has been raining **since** 5:00 p.m.

in, into, within

In = *inside (rest)* ; **into** = *motion towards* inside ; **within** = *inside the limits* :

1. Fish live **in** water.
2. The frog jumped **into** the well.
3. He is famous **within** the country.

since, from

Since is used for a *point of time* relating to *past time* and with *perfect tenses* only. But from is used with any tense except the perfect tenses in relation to *present* and future *time* ; as—

1. He has been ill **since** Monday last.
2. I began learning English **from** the age of six. *(past)*
3. The new session will begin **from** April 1. *(future)*
4. Summer vacation begins **from** May 15. *(present)*

for, before

For is used in *negative sentences for future period of time* but **before** is used in both *negative* and *affirmative* sentences for *future point of time* ; as—

1. The sun will not rise **for** an hour yet.
2. (a) The sun will not rise **before** 6:00 a.m.
   (b) The sun will rise **before** 6:00 a.m.

TEST YOURSELF

A. Supply a suitable *preposition* for each blank :

1. The old widow died .... sorrow after her husband's death.
2. .... the surprise of everyone, he failed the test.
3. Your brother is good .... English but weak .... Science.
4. The moon does not shine .... its own light.
5. The river flows .... the bridge.
6. I prefer a book .... stories .... a book .... comics.
7. The painting was made .... a master painter.
8. I am not ready to part .... this toy at all.

9. I parted .... my friend at Paris during the journey.
10. The mouse rushed out .... its hole to help the lion.
11. The mouse rushed .... its hole to be safe from the cat.
12. Our English teacher is very popular .... the students.

B. Explain the difference :

1. (a) I will return *in* an hour. =
   (b) I will return *within* an hour. =
2. (a) He came *without* any money. =
   (b) He was *without* a roof. =
3. (a) Cows live *on* grass. =
   (b) Children live *on* their parents. =
4. (a) I am anxious about the result. =
   (b) Her parents are anxious for her safety. =
5. (a) The road is *under* repairs. =
   (b) She is *under* age yet. =
6. (a) He has retired from business. =
   (b) He has retired into private life. =
7. (a) The baby sat *beside* its mother. =
   (b) Your remark is *beside* the point. =
8. (a) I differ with you on this question. =
   (b) Your theory differs from mine. =

GERUNDS AFTER PREPOSITIONS

1. He insisted to go there. (incorrect)
   He *insisted on* **going** there. (correct)
2. We must refrain to do wrong. (incorrect)
   We must *refrain from* **doing** wrong. (correct)
3. They prohibited me to do so. (incorrect)
   They *prohibited* me *from* **doing** so. (correct)
4. Don't prevent him to do his work. (incorrect)
   Don't *prevent* him *from* **doing** his work. (correct)
5. Abstain to speak foul words. (incorrect)
   Abstain from **speaking** foul words. (correct)

TEST YOURSELF

A. Explain the difference :

1. (a) I shall attend the meeting. = ...
   (b) I shall attend to the meeting. = ...

2. (a) I shall bear this difficulty. = ...
   (b) I shall not bear with this insult. = ...

3. (a) Let us begin a song. = ...
   (b) Let us begin with a song. = ...

4. (a) I will call him there. = ...
   (b) I will call on him there. = ...

5. (a) Count this money. = ...
   (b) Count on this money. = ...

6. (a) I shall deal the cards. = ...
   (b) I deal in cards. = ...

7. (a) Always eat at fixed times. = ...
   (b) Disease eats into the body. = ...

8. (a) I met an old friend of mine. = ...
   (b) I met with an accident. = ...

9. (a) Send the doctor. = ...
   (b) Send for the doctor. = ...

10. (a) He worked the machine. = ...
    (b) He worked at the machine. = ...
    (c) The machine works well. = ...

11. (a) I always get good marks. = ...
    (b) The fox could not get at the grapes. = ...
    (c) We will soon get on to the train. = ...

8 CONJUNCTIONS: IMPORTANT FACTS

We have already studied conjunctions and their kinds. In this chapter, we shall study the correct use of some common conjunctions and conjunctional phrases.

1. **as soon as**

    As soon as he heard the sad news, he wept aloud.
    (The clause with *as soon as* is the *dependent clause*.)

2. **no sooner than**

    No sooner did he hear the news *than he* wept aloud.
    (The clause with *no sooner* is the *principal clause*.)

3. **until, till**

    Both are used to denote time only, and nothing else. **Until** is better used *to begin* a sentence, whereas **till** is used *in the middle* ; as—

    1. **Until** it is dawn, I don't get out of bed.
    2. **Until** it is 6:00 p.m., I have to work.

    But—
    I waited for you **till** 4:00 p.m.
    I stayed with him **till** it was nightfall.

    ☞ Never use *not* with **until**. It means the same as not.

4. **unless = *if not***

    Never use unless with time. Use it *with some condition* only ; as—

    1. You cannot succeed **unless** you work hard.
    2. **Unless** you agree, I will not do it.

    ☞ Never use *not* with unless. It means the same as not.

5. **because**

    Because is used to express a *cause/reason* ; as—
    He failed **because** he didn't work hard.

6. **in order that = *so that***

    It is generally followed by *may/might* ; as—
    1. Men work **in order that** they *may* earn money.
    2. I took medicine **in order that** I *might* get well.

7. **since**

As a conjunction, **since** is always followed by a verb in the *past indefinite tense*; as—

1. Two years have passed **since** my mother **died**.
2. **Since** you wish it, it **shall be done**.
3. A month has passed **since I came** here.

8. **or**

This conjunction has *four* different uses :

(a) *alternative sense* ; as—

   Either you **or** your brother is to blame.

(b) *cumulative sense* ; as—

People not working on land—traders **or** teachers **or** doctors— live in towns.

(c) *to relate synonyms* ; as—

   Africa has a large number of castes **or** tribes.

(d) to give the meaning of *otherwise* ; as—

   You must work hard **or** (*otherwise*) you will fail.

9. **if**

This conjunction is used in two senses :

(a) for asking *an indirect question* ; as—

   I asked him **if** he would have a cup of tea.

(b) for expressing a *condition* ; as—

   If you make the payment, we will supply the goods.

10. **but**

It is used in the following ways :

1. It never rains **but** it pours.	(= *without*)
2. He had no choice **but** to weep.	(= *except*)
3. He is rich **but** dissatisfied.	(= *yet*)
4. There is **but** a safety sling slung on the acrobat.	(= *only*)
5. We can **but** die.	(*at most*)

11. **lest**

This conjunction = *so that + may not*. It is always followed by **should**; as—

1. Walk fast **lest** we *should* be late.

2. He worked hard **lest** he *should* fail the test.

12. as well as

It is used to add one word to another. The verb that follows it is according to the *first word/noun* ; as—

1. *He* **as well as** *you* **is** to blame.
2. *You* **as well as** *he* **are** to blame.

13. neither........nor

It is used to show *double negation*. The verb is used according to the *second word/noun* etc. ; as—

1. **Neither** *he* **nor** *you* **are** to blame.
2. **Neither** *you* **nor** *he* **is** to blame.

14. either............or

It is used like *neither..........nor* ; as—

1. **Either** *he* **or** *you* **are** to blame.
2. **Either** *you* **or** *he* **is** to blame.

TEST YOURSELF

Put the correct word in each blank :

1. I as well as you .... at fault.
2. Either this boy or his parents .... made this mistake.
3. No sooner .... the teacher step in, the students ....
4. Unless you work very hard, you .... pass the test.
5. Hold these two pigeons .... I come here again.
6. The patient took medicine in order that he .... get well.
7. Two hours .... passed since I fell fast asleep.
8. .... I am weak, I am at least intelligent.
9. They walked fast lest they .... miss the train.
10. There was no one .... wept to hear her tale of woe.

9. SPEECH—DIRECT AND INDIRECT—I

Speech—*direct* and *indirect*—explains how to report in different ways what people say or think. There are two chief ways of reporting things.

    1.   *Direct Speech (Reporting)*   2.   *Indirect Speech (Reporting)*

A. DIRECT SPEECH

One way of reporting is to **repeat the actual words spoken by another person**. Clearly, the speaker cannot express the words of another person as his/her own. So, those words have to be put within *inverted commas*.

Observe the following examples :

1. Erika said, "I do not know much about music."
2. The teacher said, "The school will remain closed tomorrow."
3. The king said, "We must give alms to the poor daily."
4. Martin said, "James is working hard."
5. The beggar said, "Give me something to eat, sir."
6. The slave said, "The lion is limping."
7. They say, "Dancing is a good exercise."

This way of reporting is called DIRECT SPEECH.

Direct speech is made up of two distinct parts :

    1.   The *Reporting* Clause   2.   The *Reported* Clause

The Reporting Clause is the part of the direct speech that is out of the inverted commas. This clause just mentions that something is going to be reported. The verb of this clause (*say*, *ask*, *tell*, etc.) is called the **reporting verb**.

The Reported Clause is the part of the direct speech that is within the inverted commas. This clause repeats the words of another person without any change.

Remember the following facts about Direct Speech :

1. The reporting verb is followed by a *comma (,)*.
2. The *inverted commas are put* after the comma.
3. Then comes the reported clause. The first word of this clause begins with a capital letter.
4. At the end of the reported clause, the inverted commas are closed.
5. The commas are always closed after the last punctuation mark—(.), (?)—or (!)—not before it in any case.

B. INDIRECT SPEECH

The other way of reporting is to **express in one's own words what another person has said**. Clearly, there is no need to put the reported clause within inverted commas.

Observe the following examples :

1. Erika said that she did not know much about music.
2. The teacher said that the school would be closed the next day.
3. The king said that they must give alms to the poor daily.
4. Martin said that James was working hard.
5. The beggar requested for something to eat.
6. The slave said that the lion was limping.
7. They say that dancing is a good exercise.

Indirect speech is also made up of two distinct parts :

1. The Reporting Clause   2. The Reported Clause

The Reporting Clause is the part of the indirect speech that introduces the reported speech. Its verb is called the *reporting verb* that takes a new form— different from the reporting verb of the direct speech.

The Reported Clause expresses the substance of the *Directly Reported* Speech *in the own words of the reporter*. That is why the report made in this manner is called the INDIRECT SPEECH.

☞ Note the following facts about the Indirect Speech :

1. The reporting verb of the Indirect Speech is generally different from the reporting verb of the Direct Speech. It changes according to the nature of the report.
2. The reported clause has no inverted commas to enclose it. It may be connected to the reporting clause through a conjunction—*that, if, whether* etc.
3. The reported clause has its **tenses**, changed according to set rules.
4. The reported clause has also its **pronouns** changed according to set rules.
5. Besides, some other words denoting *nearness* are replaced by words denoting *farness*.

Remember that in ordinary conversation, we generally use Indirect Speech for the following two reasons :

(a) It is not easy to remember the exact words of another person.
(b) It is not easy to quote the ideas of others exactly.

The Direct Speech is used where needed essentially. In stories, novels and plays, the Direct Speech makes the reading lively and full of interest.

CHANGING THE FORM OF SPEECH

A. CHANGING THE REPORTING VERB

The process of changing the form of speech is called **reporting**. In order to report something, a **reporting verb** is necessary. We use different reporting verbs while reporting. Basically the verb—**say**—is used generally while reporting what someone said, *i.e.* while reporting directly. But while reporting indirectly, this basic verb is changed as under :

1. While Reporting STATEMENTS :

While reporting a *statement*, either—**say**—is retained or it is changed into remarks—**tell, answer (reply), admit, suggest** etc. ; as—

1. She **said** that she knew little about music.
2. He never **told** *me* that he was in serious trouble.
3. The shopkeeper **answered** that the price was three pounds.
4. They **suggested** that we should leave as early as possible.

☞ NOTE : The verb—**tell**—must be followed by an *object*.

2. While Reporting QUESTIONS :

While reporting *a question*, the verb—**say**—is changed into **ask** or **enquire** ; as—

1. I **asked** him if I could stay with him.
2. She **asked** me where I was going.
3. She **enquired** how I was getting on.

☞ NOTE : The verb—**ask**—must be followed by an *object*.

3. While Reporting IMPERATIVES :

While reporting an *imperative*, the verb—**say**—is changed into **command, request, advise, suggest, warn, propose, remind** etc. ; as—

1. The officer **commanded** us to stop talking.
2. The beggar **requested** me for some food.
3. The doctor **advised** the patient to take rest.
4. Wendy **suggested** that we should go boating on Sunday.

4. While Reporting EXCLAMATIONS :

While reporting an *exclamation* or *optative sentences*, the verb—**say**—is changed into **shout, bless, wish, curse** or **pray, bid**, etc. ; as—

1. The mother **wished** that her son may live long.
2. People **prayed** that God might save their king.
3. She **shouted** in wonder that the baby was very lovable.
4. Robert **bade** his friend good-bye.

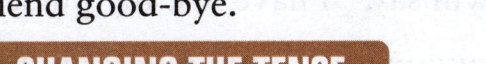

B. CHANGING THE TENSE

There are four chief rules according to which tenses change while changing a direct report into indirect report. These rules are as under :

RULE 1 If the *Reporting Verb* is in the *Present Tense* or *Future Tense*, **the tense of the** *Reported Clause does not change at all* ; as—

1. The cook says, "The dinner is ready." (*Direct*)
   The cook says that the dinner is ready. (*Indirect*)
2. The preacher will say, "Truth is evergreen." (*Direct*)
   The preacher will say that truth is evergreen. (*Indirect*)
3. Julie says, "I get up at 4-00 a.m. daily." (*Direct*)
   Julie says that she gets up at 4-00 a.m. daily. (*Indirect*)
4. The king will say, "The baby must be cut into two pieces." (*Direct*)
   The king will say that the baby must be cut into two pieces. (*Indirect*)

TEST YOURSELF

A. Change each sentence to *its indirect form* :

1. The maid says, "Tea is ready for all of you."
   ....
2. The teachers says, "The boy was lazy."
   ....
3. Mary says, "I know a lot about music."
   ....
4. Mother says, "The prices of articles are rising alarmingly."
   ....

5. The cock will say to the fox, "I am now yours, not theirs."
   ....

6. The rats say, "The cat must be belled as soon as possible."
   ....

7. Everybody says, "Walking and swimming are good for health."
   ....

8. James will say, "I have lost my purse on the way."
   ....

9. The priest says, "An earnest prayer can solve many problems."
   ....

B. Change each sentence to its *direct form* :

1. Every priest says that work is real worship.
   ....

2. George will say that he is writing a letter.
   ....

3. The slave will say that he helped the lion in the forest.
   ....

4. The zoo care-taker says that snakes are poisonous reptiles.
   ....

5. The fox will say that he wants to eat ripe grapes.
   ....

6. Richard says that Nancy loves him very dearly.
   ....

7. Tom says that there is no ink in the ink-pot.
   ....

8. Robert says that he would like to have coffee at 4-00 p.m.
   ....

9. The teacher will say that Mac will not pass.
   ....

C. Change the *form of speech* :

1. Mummy says that Mac has had his breakfast.
   ....

2. I said to Peter, "Please give me your book."
   ....
3. The pilot says that the flight will take off at 11-00 a.m.
   ....
4. Th referee says, "The match has ended in a draw."
   ....
5. I say that Russia is the best land of all.
   ....
6. The sparrow says, "I shall twitter early in the morning."
   ....

RULE 2 If the Reporting Verb is in the *past tense*, each *present tense* of the Reported Clause changes into its *corresponding past tense*, i.e.

1. *Is/am changes into was.*
2. **Have/has** changes into **had**.
3. **Present Indefinite Tense** changes into **Past Indefinite Tense**.
4. **Present Continuous Tense** changes into **Past Continuous Tense**.
5. **Present Perfect Tense** changes into **Past Perfect Tense**.
6. **Present Perfect Continuous Tense** changes into **Past Perfect Continuous Tense**.
7. (a) **can** changes into **could** (b) **may** changes into **might**
   (c) **has to** changes into **had to** (d) **is to /are to** changes into **was/were to**.

Observe the following examples :

1. *The stranger said to me, "I want to go to the bus-stop."* (Direct)
   The stranger told me that he **wanted** to go to the bus-stop. (Indirect)
2. The lawyer said, "This point **is** very difficult to prove." (Direct)
   The lawyer remarked that this point **was** very difficult to prove. (Indirect)
3. Clark said to Misty, " I **am to** kill you." (Direct)
   Clark told Misty that he **was to** kill her. (Indirect)
4. The teacher said, "Tests **are** going on." (Direct)
   The teacher remarked that tests **were** going on. (Indirect)
5. Mummy said, "Alfred **has had** a cup of milk." (Direct)
   Mummy said that Alfred **had had** a cup of milk. (Indirect)

6. They said to us, "It **has been raining** since morning.". *(Direct)*
   They told us that it **had been raining** since morning. *(Indirect)*

7. The wrestler said, "I **can** lift this heavy stone easily." *(Direct)*
   The wrestler said that he **could** lift this heavy stone easily. *(Indirect)*

8. The teacher said to me, "You **may** come in." *(Direct)*
   The teacher told me that I **might** go in. *(Indirect)*

9. He said to the teacher, "I **have to** rise very early. *(Direct)*
   He told the teacher that he **had to** rise very early. *(Indirect)*

10. The people said to the king, "We **are** your humble subjects." *(Direct)*
    The people told the king that they **were** his humble subjects. *(Indirect)*

11. Mary said, "I **have been** ill for four days." *(Direct)*
    Mary said that she **had been** ill for four days. *(Indirect)*

12. The teacher said, "This hill has a flat top." *(Direct)*
    The teacher told us that hill **had** a flat top. *(Indirect)*

TEST YOURSELF

A. Change each sentence to its *indirect form* :

1. The captain said, "We have found a true player."
   ....

2. The servant said, "I don't know much about it."
   ....

3. The coach said, "He is developing into a good forward player."
   ....

4. Gary said, "I am taking my friend down in my car."
   ....

5. Mac said, "That is all right ; but I cannot go with you."
   ....

6. He said to me, "Wait until I come."
   ....

7. The old man said, "I have a morning walk daily."
....

8. The watchman said, "Children are playing in the park."
....

9. "We have to labour very hard," said the labourers.
....

10. "It has been raining heavily since morning," said the farmer.
....

B. Change each sentence to its *direct form* :

1. Thomas remarked that he could not solve that sum.
....

2. The leader of the pigeons said that they had to fly along with the net.
....

3. The mouse said that the lion was roaring aloud in despair.
....

4. The slave told the people that he had lived in the lion's cave.
....

5. The mother said that everyone could have a chocolate.
....

RULE 3. If the Reporting Verb is in the *past tense*, the *past tenses of the Reported Clause* change as under :

1. **Was/were changes into had been.**
2. **Past Indefinite Tense changes into Past Perfect Tense.**
3. **Past Continuous Tense changes into Past Perfect Continuous Tense.**
4. **Past Perfect Tense and Past Perfect Continuous Tense do not change at all.**

Observe the following examples :

1. The king said, "The cricket **was** out of its web." (Direct)
   The king remarked that the cricket **had been** out of its web. (Indirect)

2. The slave said, "The lion **was** limping." (Direct)
   The slave remarked that the lion **had been** limping. (Indirect)

TEST YOURSELF

3. The teacher told us, "King Bruce **had hidden** in a cave." (*Direct*)
   The teacher told us that King Bruce **had hidden** in a cave. (*Indirect*)

4. Alfred said, "It **had been raining** since morning." (*Direct*)
   Alfred said that it **had been raining** since morning. (*Indirect*)

A. Change each sentence to its *indirect form* :

1. James said to us, "I was out of town on Monday."
   ....
2. The policeman said, "The burglar was caught on Sunday."
   ....
3. The king said, "The soldier deserves a prize."
   ....
4. Mother told me, "It had been snowing for an hour."
   ....
5. The station-master said, "The train had left on time."
   ....
6. The peon said, "The children were making a noise."
   ....
7. The beggar said, "The king had not given me anything."
   ....
8. Mac said, "I found the job difficult."
   ....
9. The client said to the lawyer, "I wanted your opinion on it."
   ....

B. Change each sentence to *direct form of speech* :

1. The officer told us that the thief had been arrested.
   ....
2. The referee remarked that the hare had lost the race.
   ....
3. The old lady said that girls had been singing melodious songs.
   ....

4. Peter said that it had been rainning since evening.
   ....

5. Clark told his brother that he had killed the demon.
   ....

6. The king remarked that he had been doing justice.
   ....

C. Change the *form of speech* **:**

1. Misty said, "Angelina went home at 2-00 p.m."
   ....

2. The mother said that the baby had been weeping bitterly for milk.
   ....

3. The cat said, "A hare and a tortoise were running a race."
   ....

4. The student said that the teacher had been teaching a new lesson that day.
   ....

5. "Weather had been very inclement for many days," said the scientist.
   ....

6. The king told his ministers, "The cricket had made nine attempts."
   ....

RULE 4 If the Reporting Verb is in the *past tense,* all future tenses have their *shall and will* changed into *would* :

Observe the following examples :

1. *Mary said, "Tom will make tea for us all."* (Direct)
   Mary remarked that Tom would make tea for all of them. (Indirect)

2. They said, "We shall take a test on Monday." (Direct)
   They said that they would take a test on Monday. (Indirect)

3. The crow said to the fox, "I'll sing a song." (Direct)
   The crow told the fox that it would sing a song. (Indirect)

TEST YOURSELF

A. Change each sentence to its *indirect form* :

1. He said, "When will the train start ?"
   ....

2. The cricket said, "I must get to my web this time."
   ....

3. The slave said, "The lion will not attack me."
   ....

4. The boy said, "I will have got through the examination."
   ....

5. The priest said, "Truth will have overcome in the long run."
   ....

6. The mouse said to the lion, "I'll nibble the net and free you."
   ....

7. The children said, "We shall be enjoying swing-rides in the park."
   ....

8. Our leader said, "We shall be having a good time there."
   ....

9. The servant said, "It will have rained for 2 hours by noon."
   ....

10. The robber said to the priest, "You will not advise me any more."
    ....

B. Change each sentence to its *direct form* :

1. The soldier said that the king would be hiding in a cave.
   ....

2. Alice said that Lucy would look after her sons.
   ....

3. The scientist said that the sun would have set at 6-20 p.m.
   ....

4. The teacher said that all the students would get through.
   ....

5. The cook assured the master that the food would be ready soon.
   ....

6. The beggar blessed me saying that God would bless me.
   ....

7. The old man remarked that the sky would be overcast with clouds.
   ....

C. Change the *form of speech* :

1. The officer said to the typist, "You shall type this letter just now."
   ....

2. The robber said to the traveller that he would snatch everything from him.
   ....

3. The child said to its mother, "I'll have a chocolate."
   ....

4. The wife remarked that she would buy a new dress.
   ....

5. The priest said, "The sun will never rise in the west."
   ....

6. The woodcutter said to the angel that he would take his own axe only.
   ....

7. The teacher said to the students, "I'll teach you a new lesson tomorrow."
   ....

10 SPEECH—DIRECT AND INDIRECT—II

We studied in the previous lesson about—
- (a) the two ways of reporting—**direct** and **indirect**.
- (b) the **reporting clause** and **reported clause**.
- (c) how **tenses change** while *changing direct reports into indirect reports*.

In this lesson, we shall learn more about the two ways of reporting—
- (a) How **pronouns change** while changing direct reports into indirect reports.
- (b) How **words denoting nearness** change into **words denoting farness**.

CHANGE IN PRONOUNS

There are **four chief rules** that govern the change of pronouns when direct reports are changed into indirect reports.

RULE 1 Pronouns of the *First Person* in the Reported Clause change after the *Person of the Subject* of the *Reporting Verb* ; as—

1. *Raju* said to me, "I have done **my** homework." (*Direct*)
   Raju told me that **he** had done **his** homework. (*Indirect*)
2. *I* said to her, "I have had **my** breakfast." (*Direct*)
   I told her that **I** had had **my** breakfast. (*Indirect*)
3. *You* said to him, "I do not fear anybody." (*Direct*)
   You told him that **you** did not fear anybody. (*Indirect*)

In these sentences—

1. The **subject** of the Reporting Verb is **John** (*Third Person*). So, **I** of the Reported Clause changed into **he** and *my* into **his**.
2. The **subject** of the Reporting Verb is **I** (*First Person*). So, **I** of the Reported Clause **remained unchanged**.
3. The **subject** of the Reporting Verb is **you** (*Second Person*). So, **I** of the Reported Clause became **you**.

RULE 2 The pronoun WE (*First Person*) remains unchanged when it indicates *mankind* or when it includes both the *speaker* and the *listener* ; as—

A. When WE stands for *Mankind* :

1. They say, "**We** are toys in the hands of Fate." (*Direct*)
   They say that we are toys in the hands of Fate. (*Indirect*)

2. The priest said, "**We** must never tell lies." (*Direct*)
   The priest remarked that **we** must never tell lies. (*Indirect*)

B. When WE includes the *Speaker* and the *Listener* :

1. He said, "**We** must face this problem boldly. (*Direct*)
   He remarked that **we** must face this problem boldly. (*Indirect*)
2. He said to me, "**We** both are to blame." (*Direct*)
   He told me that **we** both were to blame. (*Indirect*)

RULE 3 Pronouns of the *Second Person* in the Reported Clause change after the *Person of the Object* of the Reporting Verb ; as—

1. She said to *me*, "**You** are not punctual." (*Direct*)
   She told *me* that **I** was not punctual. (*Indirect*)
2. I said to *him*, "I like **you** very much." (*Direct*)
   I told *him* that I liked **him** very much. (*Indirect*)
3. He said to *you*, "**You** are late." (*Direct*)
   He told you that **you** were late. (*Indirect*)

In these sentences—

1. The **object** of the Reporting Verb is **me** (*First Person*). So, **you** of the Reported Clause changed into **I**.
2. The **object** of the Reporting Verb is **him** (*Third Person*). So, **you** of the Reported Clause became **him**.
3. The **object** of the Reporting Verb is **you** (*Second Person*). So, **you** of the Reported Clause **remained unchanged**.

RULE 4 Pronouns of the *Third Person* **remain unchanged** ; as—

1. I said, "**He** is honest and sincere." (*Direct*)
   I remarked that **he** was honest and sincere. (*Indirect*)
2. They said, "**She** will not recover soon." (*Direct*)
   They remarked that **she** would not recover soon. (*Indirect*)
3. Mummy said, "**They** are idle and lazy.." (*Direct*)
   Mummy remarked that **they** were idle and lazy. (*Indirect*)

In these sentences—

1. **He** of the Reported Clause has remained **he**.
2. **She** of the Reported Clause has remained **she**.
3. **They** of the Reported Clause has remained **they**.

TEST YOURSELF

A. Change each sentence to *its indirect form* :

1. The farmer said, "I have killed the snake."
   ....
2. She said to me, "You have misbehaved with me."
   ....
3. You said openly, "I am not in favour of this plan."
   ....
4. I said, "She is tall, slim and fair."
   ....
5. They said to us, "We all are fond of milk."
   ....
6. They said, "We are mortals."
   ....
7. The leader said to his men, "We must march ahead."
   ....
8. She said to me, "You are no less than an idiot."
   ....
9. The teacher said, "The sun is stationary in relation to the earth."
   ....

B. Change each sentence to its *direct form* :

1. He told me that I was late.
   ....
2. You told him that he had failed the test.
   ....
3. Jennifer told Emma that she looked smart.
   ....
4. I told him that I would return on Saturday.
   ....
5. I said that I was alright.
   ....

6. You told her that you were awfully busy.
   ....

7. Clark remarked that he had been ill for four days.
   ....

8. Gary told Steve that he had killed the witch.
   ....

9. I remarked that I was fond of bread and butter.
   ....

10. The customer told the shopkeeper that he would have less to count.
    ....

C. Change the form of *speech* :

1. The teacher said, "I will teach a new lesson tomorrow."
   ....

2. The teacher said to me, "You must be regular in your studies."
   ....

3. He admitted that it was we who were to blame.
   ....

4. The hare told the lion that another lion had detained him on the way.
   ....

5. James told Mac that he had never seen such a picture ever before.
   ....

6. The shopkeeper said to the customer, "You will have less to carry."
   ....

7. Alfred said to his sister, "I shall have a cup of coffee."
   ....

8. The innkeeper told the traveller that he had lost the silver key.
   ....

9. The clerk told the officer that his testimonials were enclosed with his application.
   ....

10. Mary said to her friend, "I have a little black lamb."
    ....

RULE 5 When the *present tense* of the Reported Speech changes into *past tense*, words expressing *nearness* are changed into those *showing farness*; as—

1.	**ago**	into	**before**	6.	**this**	into	**that**
2.	**here**	into	**there**	7.	**these**	into	**those**
3.	**hither**	into	**thither**	8.	**today**	into	**that day**
4.	**hence**	into	**thence**	9.	**tonight**	into	**that night**
5.	**hereby**	into	**thereby**	10.	**come**	into	**go** (*seldom*)

11. **last night/week/month/year** into **previous night/week/month/year**
12. **next day/week/month/year** into **following day/week/month/year**
13. **yesterday** into **the previous day**
14. **tomorrow** into **the following/next day**

Observe the following examples :

1. My brother said, "We shall watch a film *tonight*." (*Direct*)
   My brother remarked that they would watch a film **that night**. (*Indirect*)

2. The traveller said, "I was dead tired *yesterday*." (*Direct*)
   The traveller remarked that he had been dead tired **the previous day**. (*Indirect*)

3. My friend said to me, "I'll see you *tomorrow*." (*Direct*)
   My friend told me that he would see me **the following day**. (*Indirect*)

4. My servant said to me, "I shall do all *these* jobs well." (*Direct*)
   My servant told me that he would do all **those** jobs well. (*Indirect*)

5. My friend said to me, "What has made you laugh like *this*." (*Direct*)
   My friend asked me what had made me laugh like **that**. (*Indirect*)

6. He ordered me, "Do it *now* and *here*." (*Direct*)
   He ordered me to do it **then** and **there**. (*Indirect*)

7. My uncle said, "I shall visit New York *next week*." (*Direct*)
   My uncle remarked that he would visit New York **the following week**. (*Indirect*)

TEST YOURSELF

A. Change each sentence to its *indirect speech* :

1. The labourer said, "It is very hot and stuffy today."

   ....

2. The teacher said to him, "You may see me tomorrow."
   ....

3. The monitor said, "This sum is not very difficult."
   ....

4. James said to Williams, "I came to see you yesterday."
   ....

5. Mark said to Jake, "I had come here two years ago."
   ....

6. The fruiterer said, "These mangoes are ripe and juicy."
   ....

7. The officer said, "I'll come to see you the next week."
   ....

8. The angel said, "Martin ! your name is not there in this book."
   ....

9. My friend said to me, "Here is your lost pen."
   ....

10. The letter read, "The point raised is hereby explained as follows."
    ....

B. Change each sentence to its *direct speech* :

1. The farmer said that it looked like rain that day.
   ....

2. The teacher said that the class would go for a picnic the next day.
   ....

3. Mac told me that he intended to see me the next day.
   ....

4. Alfred said that his father had died two years before.
   ....

5. The accountant remarked that the debt would amount to one thousand two years hence.
   ....

11 SPEECH—DIRECT AND INDIRECT—III

We learnt about the changes in **tenses**, changes in *pronouns* and changes in **certain words** while converting *direct reports* into *indirect reports*.

Here in this chapter we shall study how to change **statements** and **imperative sentences** from direct form to indirect form and vice versa.

CONVERSION OF STATEMENTS

While converting directly reported statements (assertive sentences) into indirect reports, we must follow the rules given as under :

1. Change the *reporting verb*—**say**—into **remark** or it *remains unchanged* if there is *no object* after it.
2. Change the *reporting verb*—**say**—into **tell**—if there is *an object* after it.
3. Remove *comma* and *inverted commas* and put the conjunction—**that**—to connect the reporting clause with the reported clause.
4. Change the tenses according to the rules explained in the previous chapter.
5. Change the personal pronouns according to the rules already explained.
6. Nouns or Pronouns at the **vocative case** (*used for addressing a person*) are treated as objects of the reporting verbs.
7. Words denoting *nearness* are changed into words denoting *farness*.
8. Other general rules are also followed.

Observe the following examples :

A. FROM DIRECT TO INDIRECT

1. The king said, "My people must be kept happy." (*Direct*)
   The king **remarked** that his people must be kept happy. (*Indirect*)
2. Both the friends said, "We shall face every danger together." (*Direct*)
   Both the friends **pledged** that they would face every danger together. (*Indirect*)
3. Smith said to me, "I differ with you on this point." (*Direct*)
   Smith **told** me that he differed with me on that point. (*Indirect*)
4. Daddy said to me, "You look just like your mother." (*Direct*)
   Daddy **told** me that I looked just like my mother. (*Indirect*)

B. INDIRECT TO DIRECT

While changing statements from Indirect Speech to its Direct Form the rules mentioned above are reversed.

Observe the following examples :

1. The teacher told the pupil that he was much too lazy. *(Indirect)*
   The teacher said to the pupil, "You are much too lazy." *(Direct)*
2. My friend told me that he did not like my habits. *(Indirect)*
   My friend said to me, "I do not like your habits." *(Direct)*
3. The teacher remarked that he would teach a new lesson. *(Indirect)*
   The teacher said, "I shall teach a new lesson." *(Direct)*

TEST YOURSELF

A. Change each sentence to *indirect form of speech* :

1. The priest said, "The girl was too young to be married."
   ....
2. The innkeeper told the traveller, "I have found the key."
   ....
3. She said to me, "I have learnt that the writer of this story is dead."
   ....
4. He said, "I don't believe that she hates me."
   ....
5. Gary thought, "I must go and see Jonathan just now."
   ....
6. The late-comer said, "I am extremely sorry for being late."
   ....
7. Bruce said to himself, "I must keep trying."
   ....
8. The guest said, "I knocked at the door and was let in."
   ....
9. Michael said, "He isn't a bad chap after all."
   ....

B. Change each sentence to *direct form of speech* :

1. I told her that I was so glad she had come.
   ....

2. I told my officer that I was to go home early.
   ....
3. The passenger told the policeman that he was aware of that danger.
   ....
4. The soldier remarked that they were only three but they could face three hundred.
   ....
5. The teacher told me that I was very careless about my studies.
   ....
6. Tina told her friend that she would stand by him through thick and thin.
   ....
7. The gardener remarked that he would weed those plants.
   ....
8. The host told his guests that they could stay with him.
   ....
9. The police told the thief that he had been caught red-handed at last.
   ....

C. Change the *form of sentence* :

1. Clark said, "Mother, you are so kind to me and I can never forget you."
   ....
2. The priest remarked that God would bless me in every way.
   ....
3. The doctor said to the patient, "You need complete rest for a month."
   ....
4. The teacher told the class that he would teach a new lesson the following day.
   ....
5. The traffic policeman said, "Nobody should cross the road carelessly."
   ....
6. I told my friend that I had been to the Eiffel Tower several times.
   ....
7. The child said that the sun was just overhead at that time.
   ....
8. The old woman told her only son, "Do take exercise regularly."
   ....

9. The leader of the pigeons said, "We must fly away holding the net in our beaks."

....

CONVERSION OF IMPERATIVE SENTENCES

While changing **imperative sentences** from *direct* to *indirect form*, observe the rules given below :

1. The reporting verb—**say**—is changed into **order/command**—if the sentence expresses a *command*.
2. the reporting verb—**say**—is changed into—**pray/request**—if the sentence expresses a *request*
3. The reporting verb—**say**—is changed into—**advise/instruct**—if the sentence expresses an *advice*.
4. The reporting verb—**say**—is changed into—**warn**—if the sentence expresses a *warning*.
5. The reporting verb—**say**—is changed into—**suggest/propose**—if the sentence expresses a *proposal*.
6. The comma and the inverted commas after the reporting verb are removed.
7. **To/Not to** is used to connect the reporting clause with the reported clause.
8. Nouns and pronouns in the vocative case are treated as the objects of the reporting verbs.
9. *Tenses* and *personal pronouns* and *words of nearness* are changed according to their respective rules.
10. Other general rules are also observed.

A. FROM DIRECT TO INDIRECT

Observe the following examples :

1. The master said to the servant, "Do it at once." *(Direct)*
   The master ordered the servant to do it at once. *(Indirect)*
2. The king said to the minister, "Look after my people well." *(Direct)*
   The king instructed the minister to look after his people well. *(Indirect)*
3. The mother said to her son, " Do not tell lies." *(Direct)*
   The mother advised her son not to tell lies. *(Indirect)*

4.	The doctor said to the patient, "Don't eat fried food."	(*Direct*)
	The doctor forbade the patient to eat fried food.	(*Indirect*)
5.	The beggar said to me, "Give me something to eat."	(*Direct*)
	The beggar requested me to give him something to eat.	(*Indirect*)
6.	The teacher said to the students, "Don't be careless of your studies."	(*Direct*)
	The teacher warned the students not to be careless of their studies.	(*Indirect*)
7.	Clark said to us, "Let us go swimming in the canal."	(*Direct*)
	Clark proposed that we should go swimming in the canal.	(*Indirect*)

B. FROM INDIRECT TO DIRECT

1.	The servant requested his master to pardon him for his fault.	(*Indirect*)
	The servant said to his master, "Pardon me for my fault, sir."	(*Direct*)
2.	The queen ordered her maid to make her bed at once.	(*Indirect*)
	The queen said to her maid, "Make my bed at once."	(*Direct*)
3.	The physician advised the patient to take liquid food for two days at least.	(*Indirect*)
	The physician said to the patient, "Take liquid food for two days at least."	(*Direct*)
4.	The boatman warned the boy not to go into deep water.	(*Indirect*)
	The boatman said to the boy, "Don't go into deep water."	(*Direct*)
5.	Mac suggested that we should go boating on Sunday.	(*Indirect*)
	Mac said to us, "Let us go boating on Sunday."	(*Direct*)

TEST YOURSELF

A. Change each sentence to its *indirect speech* :

1. The lawyer said to the witness, "Say as I have told you."
   ....
2. She said to her friend, "Let us dance in the room."
   ....
3. The father said, "Don't waste your time, my son."
   ....
4. The officer said to the peon, "Carry this file to the clerk."
   ....

5. Stella said to Steve, "Lend me your book, please."
   ....
6. Alfred said to the officer, "Let me go home, sir."
   ....
7. I said to my friend, "Let us go for a picnic."
   ....
8. James said, "Pardon me this time, dad. I'll never disobey you again."
   ....
9. Mac said to Sally, "Hold these pigeons and stay here till I come back."
   ....

B. Change each sentence to its *direct form* :

1. The beggar requested the lady respectfully to give him food to eat.
   ....
2. The teacher advised the students to attend to the lesson.
   ....
3. The father advised his son not to do that again.
   ....
4. The wolf warned the lamb not to make the water muddy.
   ....
5. The priest directed me to do as he did.
   ....
6. The robber threatened me to give him whatever I had.
   ....
7. The mistress ordered her maid to pack up her things and be off.
   ....
8. The culprit requested the judge to let him meet his children for the last time.
   ....
9. The manager warned the peon not to disturb him again and again.
   ....

C. Change the *form of speech* :

1. I requested him not to beat me again.
   ....
2. The principal said to the clerk, "Let the student come in."
   ....
3. The father advised his children to get up early every day.
   ....

12 SPEECH—DIRECT AND INDIRECT—IV

In the previous chapter, we learnt how to change *assertive* and *imperative* sentences from Direct to Indirect form of speech and vice versa. In this lesson, we shall study how to change **interrogative sentences** from one form of speech to another.

We know that interrogative sentences are of two types. We read about them in chapter 1 on page 5. These two types of interrogative sentences are as under :

1. Those beginning with **Helping Verbs**.
2. Those beginning with **Question Words**.

There are different rules for changing these two types of interrogative sentences from one form of speech to another. Let us first study the conversion of Interrogative Sentences that begin with helping verbs.

CONVERSION OF INTERROGATIVE SENTENCES (BEGINNING WITH AUXILIARY VERBS)

Here are the rules :

1. The Reporting Verb—**say**—is changed into **ask** or **enquire** if there is an object after it. But if there is no object, only the verb—**enquire**—is used in place of—**say**.
2. The comma after the Reporting Verb and the inverted commas are removed and **if** or **whether** is used to join the Reporting Clause and the Reported Clause.
3. The *interrogative form* of the Reported Clause is changed to its **assertive form**.
4. Nouns or Pronouns in the vocative case are treated as objects of the Reporting Verb.
5. Other general rules are also observed.
6. Nouns or Pronouns in the **vocative case** (*used for addressing a person*) are treated as objects of the reporting verbs.
7. Words denoting *nearness* are changed into words denoting *farness*.
8. Other general rules are also followed.

Observe the following examples :

A. FROM DIRECT TO INDIRECT

1. Tina said to me, "Are you unwell ?" *(Direct)*
   Tina asked me if I was unwell. *(Indirect)*

2. Mac asked James, "Do you take exercise regularly? *(Direct)*
   Mac enquired of James if he took exercise regularly. *(Indirect)*

3. The host said to the guest, "Would you have tea or coffee? *(Direct)*
   The host asked the guest whether he would have tea or coffee. *(Indirect)*

4. The jackal said to the fox, "Are the grapes sweet ?" *(Direct)*
   The jackal enquired of the fox whether the grapes were sweet. *(Indirect)*

5. Gary said, "May I use your pen, Mike ?" *(Direct)*
   Gary asked Mike if he might use his pen. *(Indirect)*

B. INDIRECT TO DIRECT

While changing statements from Indirect Speech to its Direct Form the rules mentioned above are reversed.

Observe the following examples :

1. The clerk asked the officer respectfully if he might go in. *(Indirect)*
   The clerk said to the officer, "May I come in, sir ?" *(Direct)*

2. The crow enquired of the fox whether he wanted that cheese. *(Indirect)*
   The crow said to the fox, "Do you want this cheese, Mr Fox ?" *(Direct)*

3. Jane asked Julie whether she had taken her share. *(Indirect)*
   Jane said to Julie, "Have you taken your share ?" *(Direct)*

4. The guide enquired of us whether we needed his help. *(Indirect)*
   The guide said to us, "Do you need my help ?" *(Direct)*

TEST YOURSELF

A. Change each sentence to its *indirect form* :

1. She said to me, "Are your parents alive ?"

   ....

2. The gateman said to him, "Have you got an entry ticket?"
   ....

3. I said to my friend, "Do you believe in God or not?"
   ....

4. The policeman said to us, "May I help you in any way?"
   ....

5. Someone said to me, "Is the work going on well?"
   ....

6. Misty said to James, "Would you stay at her house or at a hotel?"
   ....

7. The general asked his soldier, "Are you ready to die for your country?"
   ....

8. The husband said to his wife, "Is the dinner ready?"
   ....

9. The child said to its grandmother, "Will you tell me the story of the honest woodcutter?"
   ....
   ....

10. The shopkeeper said to the customer, "Will you have a cold drink or a hot one?"
    ....

B. **Change each sentence to its *direct form* :**

1. The policeman asked the youth if he was Edward, the scientist.
   ....

2. I enquired of my friend if he would dine with us the following day.
   ....

3. Misty enquired of David whether he had done his homework or not.
   ....

4. The teacher asked Peter if he had abused Sam the previous day.
   ....

5. Mac asked James whether he would accompany him to the forest.
   ....

6. The students enquired of the teacher if he had marked their answer-sheets or not.
   ....
   ....

7. Anna asked her sister if she would go to the movie alone.
   ....

8. The servant asked his master if he should open the window.
   ....

9. The traveller asked the policeman if he could tell him the way to the nearest hotel.
   ....

10. I asked Della whether she wanted to go with us for picnic.
    ....

C. Change the *form of speech* :

1. The lady said to the gateman, "Did you see my brother anywhere?"
   ....

2. The doctor asked the patient, "Are you taking the medicine regularly?"
   ....

3. The teacher said to the students, "Can't you keep quiet ?"
   ....

4. My uncle asked me, "Will you like to have a present on your birthday?"
   ....

5. The servant said to his master, "May I get leave for a month as I want to go to my village ?"
   ....
   ....

6. The wolf asked the crane if he would take out the bone stuck up in his throat.
   ....

7. Alexander said to Porus, "Should I treat you as a king treats another king ?"
   ....

8. The beggar said to the rich man, "Will you please help me with some money ?"
....

9. Mary said to the lamb, "Will you follow me wherever I go ?"
....

10. The traveller said to the innkeeper, "Have you really lost the silver key ?"
....

CONVERSION OF INTERROGATIVE SENTENCES
(BEGINNING WITH QUESTION WORDS)

Here are the rules :

1. The Reporting Verb—**say**—is changed into **ask** or **enquire** as in the other type of interrogative sentences.
2. Remove the commas after the Reporting Verb and also the inverted commas.
3. No conjunction is used to connect the Reporting Clause with the Reported Clause.
4. Change the interrogative form of the sentence into its assertive form.
5. Nouns and Pronouns of the *vocative case* are treated as objects of the reporting verbs.
6. Other general rules are also carried out.

Observe the following examples :

A. FROM DIRECT TO INDIRECT

1. *The mother said to Joe, "Why did you beat my son ?"* (Direct)
   The mother asked Joe why he had beaten her son. (Indirect)

2. *My uncle said to me, "What present would you have on your birthday ?"* (Direct)
   My uncle asked me what present I would have on my birthday. (Indirect)

3. *She said to me, " What do you want after all ?"* (Direct)
   She asked me what I wanted after all. (Indirect)

4. The officer said to the clerk, "Why have you come late ?" *(Direct)*
   The officer enquired of the clerk why he had come late. *(Indirect)*

5. The stranger said to me, "What is your name ?" *(Direct)*
   The stranger asked me what my name was. *(Indirect)*

6. James said to me, "How did you do this sum ?" *(Direct)*
   James asked me how I had done that sum. *(Indirect)*

7. The officer asked the peon, "Why do you disturb me again and again." *(Direct)*
   The officer asked the peon why he disturbed him again and again. *(Indirect)*

B. FROM INDIRECT TO DIRECT

1. The husband asked his wife why she could not accompany him. *(Indirect)*
   The husband said to his wife, "Why can't you accompany me?" *(Direct)*

2. The father asked his son why he did not get up early. *(Indirect)*
   The father said to his son, "Why don't you get up early?" *(Direct)*

3. The new teacher asked the class who their monitor was. *(Indirect)*
   The new teacher said to the class, "Who is your monitor?" *(Direct)*

4. The customer asked the shopkeeper why he had cheated him. *(Indirect)*
   The customer said to the shopkeeper, "Why did you cheat me?" *(Direct)*

5. The lion asked the hare what had caused him reach there late. *(Indirect)*
   The lion said to the hare, "What caused you reach here late?" *(Direct)*

TEST YOURSELF

A. Change each sentence to its *indirect speech* :

1. The father said to the teacher, "How is my son getting on ?"
   ....

2. My friend said to me, "Which way are you going ?"
   ....

3. The policeman came and said, "What has happened ?"
   ....

4. I asked my friends, "How did you like the new film ?"
   ....

5. The principal said to me, "Why are you so late ?"
   ....

6. I said to the children, "Who has put my book here ?"
   ....

7. My father asked us, "What are you talking about ?"
   ....

8. The mother asked her daughter, "How have you made your clothes dirty so soon ?"
   ....

9. The officer asked the clerk, "Where do you live and how do you come to office ?"
   ....

10. The slim friend said to his fat friend, "Why are you angry with me ? Have you taken my words seriously ?"
    ....
    ....

B. Change each sentence to its *direct form* :

1. The old farmer asked his sons why they could not work together.
   ....

2. The father asked his son why he couldn't see that he had grown very old and weak.
   ....

3. The master asked his servant why he disturbed him again and again.
   ....

4. The teacher asked me what my father was.
   ....

5. They asked me what made me laugh so loudly.
   ....

6. I asked my uncle what he wanted me to do after all.
   ....

7. The stranger asked the policeman which was the shortest way to the railway-station.
   ....

8. The doctor asked the patient how he felt then and when he had taken his last dose.
   ....

9. The old widow asked his youthful son why he did not do some work to earn money.
   ....

10. The rich man asked the beggar what forced him to beg and how he could leave begging.
    ....

C. Change the *form of speech* :

1. The queen asked the maid why she had not made her bed.
   ....

2. The father said to his son, "Why haven't you got ready for school so far ?"
   ....

3. Clark asked his grandfather why he had called him and what he could do for him.
   ....

4. The teacher asked Sally why she looked sad and whether her mother had not recovered from illness.
   ....
   ....

5. The principal said to the student, "What is your father and why do you want a concession in fees ?"
   ....
   ....

13 SPEECH—DIRECT AND INDIRECT—V

We have already learnt how to change *assertive, imperative* and *interrogative* sentences from Direct to Indirect form of speech and vice versa. In this lesson, we shall study how to change **optative** and **exclamatory sentences** from one form of speech to another.

CONVERSION OF OPTATIVE SENTENCES

We know that optative sentences express :

1. *Wishes*   2. *Blessings*   3. *Prayers*   4. *Curses*

So, while reporting optative sentences indirectly, these rules are to be observed :

1. Change the Reporting Verb into—**wish, bless, pray** or **curse** according to what the Direct Report expresses.
2. Change the *optative form* of the sentence into **assertive form**.
3. Remove the commas after the Reporting Verb and the inverted commas as well.
4. Use the conjunction—**that**—to connect the Reporting Clause with the Reported Speech.
5. Change the **tenses, pronouns** and **other words** according to the rules which you have already studied.
6. Treat the **vocatives** as objects of the Reporting Verbs.
7. Carry out **other general rules** as well.

Observe the following examples :

A. FROM DIRECT TO INDIRECT

1. The poor man said, "If I were a millionaire !" (*Direct*)
   The poor man **wished** that he had been a millionaire. (*Indirect*)
2. The old mother said, "May you live long, my son !" (*Direct*)
   The old mother **blessed** her son that he might live long. (*Indirect*)
3. The people said in one voice, "May God save our king !" (*Direct*)
   The people **prayed** that God might save their king. (*Indirect*)

100

4. The beggar said to the rich man, "May you be doomed !" (*Direct*)
   The beggar cursed the rich man that he might be doomed. (*Indirect*)
5. Christina said, "May I use your pen, Robert ?" (*Direct*)
   Christina asked Robert if she might use his pen. (*Indirect*)

B. INDIRECT TO DIRECT

1. The poor lad wished that he had been a prince. (*Indirect*)
   The poor lad said, "Would that I were a prince !" (*Direct*)
   or
   The poor lad said, "If I were a prince !"
2. The old man blessed his son that he might prosper. (*Indirect*)
   The old man said, "May you prosper, my son !" (*Direct*)
3. The priest prayed that God might bless the couple with a son. (*Indirect*)
   The priest said to the couple, "May God bless you with a son !" (*Direct*)
4. The old man cursed the robber that he might become a leper. (*Indirect*)
   The old man said to the robber, "May you become a leper !" (*Direct*)

TEST YOURSELF

A. Change each sentence to its *indirect form* :

1. The old lady said to the boy, "May you enjoy life in every way !"
   ....
2. The poor man said, "Would that I were also a king !"
   ....
3. The people said in one voice, "Victory to our king !"
   ....
4. The gathering said, "May the departed soul rest in peace !"
   ....
5. The oppressed slave said to his master, "May you meet the same ill fate!"
   ....
6. The priest said to the sinner, "May God pardon you !"
   ....
7. The miser said, "O that I had heaps of gold !"
   ....

8. The leader said, "May there be peace everywhere !"
   ....

9. "Halt !" shouted the officer to his men.
   ....

10. The father said to his son, "May you be safe from all dangers !"
    ....

B. Change each sentence to its *direct form* :

1. The old queen wished that the new king might live long.
   ....

2. The people prayed to God that he might save their leader.
   ....

3. The oppressed slave cursed his master that he might be doomed.
   ....

4. The priest blessed the man that he might prosper soon.
   ....

5. King Bruce wished that he had been successful like the cricket.
   ....

6. The shivering old lady earnestly prayed for a cup of hot tea.
   ....

7. The dying solider earnestly longed for a cup of water.
   ....

8. Our teacher prayed that his class might show a good result.
   ....

9. The charming girl wished that she had been a princess.
   ....

10. The soldiers prayed that the soul of their valiant general might rest in peace.
    ....

C. Change the *form of speech* :

1. The wounded patriot prayed that he might see his country free.
   ....

2. We all wished that our old mother might recover soon.
   ....

3. The father said to his son, "May you be healthy and wealthy!"
   ....

4. The king wished that there might prevail perfect peace and prosperity in his entire kingdom.
   ....
   ....

5. God be with you during your dark hour!" said the dying father to his son.
   ....

6. The poor beggar said, "If only I had been a king!"
   ....

7. The old mother blessed her son that he might come out with flying colours.
   ....

8. The invalid beggar cursed the man, "May you be helpless just like me!"
   ....

9. The dying solider wished that he might see his native land before leaving the world.
   ....

10. The unemployed youth said, "O that I could find work to do!"
    ....

CONVERSION OF EXCLAMATORY SENTENCES

We know that exclamatory sentences express strong feelings that are expressed by exclaiming a word or words under the force of those feelings. The words, we know, are based on our feelings of certain situations in every day life which are as under :

1. *joy* 2. *grief* 3. *wonder* 4. *regret* 5. *praise*
6. *anger* 7. *contempt* 8. *love (approval)* 9. *confession* 10. *rebuke*

So, the following rules have to be observed while reporting exclamatory sentences indirectly :

1. The Reporting Verb—**say**—is changed into—**exclaim**—followed by an adverb showing the feeling expressed in the sentence.

2. Sometimes the Reporting Verb—**say**—is directly changed into regret, wonder, praise, confess, rebuke, condemn, shout, greet, bid etc.
3. The exclamatory form of the sentence is changed into its assertive form.
4. The tenses and the pronouns are changed according to their rules.
5. Incomplete sentences are duly completed.

Observe the following examples :

A. FROM DIRECT TO INDIRECT

1. The queen said, "What a lovable child it is !" (*Direct*)
   The queen exclaimed in wonder that the child was very lovable. (*Indirect*)

2. The widow said, "Alas ! my husband is no more." (*Direct*)
   The widow exclaimed sorrowfully that her husband was no more. (*Indirect*)

3. The players said, " Hurrah ! we have won the match." (*Direct*)
   The players exclaimed joyfully that they had won the match. (*Indirect*)

4. The general said, "Bravo ! well done, my soldiers !" (*Direct*)
   The general praised his soldiers saying that they had done well. (*Indirect*)

5. The doctor said, "Pooh ! how dirty a child !" (*Direct*)
   The doctor exclaimed hatefully that the child was very dirty. (*Indirect*)

6. The host said, "Welcome ! come in my friends !" (*Direct*)
   The host greeted his guests with a welcome and asked them to come in. (*Indirect*)

7. "Good morning, children !" said the teacher. (*Direct*)
   The teacher wished the children good morning. (*Indirect*)

8. "Hello ! how are you, Martin ?" said Steve. (*Direct*)
   Steve greeted Martin with a hello and asked him how he was. (*Indirect*)

9. "Good-bye, friends ! God be with you !" said the host. (*Direct*)
   The host bade his guests good-bye and prayed that God be with them. (*Indirect*)

B. FROM INDIRECT TO DIRECT

1. The queen exclaimed in wonder that the rose was very beautiful. (*Indirect*)
   The queen said, "How beautiful the rose is !" (*Direct*)

2. Della exclaimed joyfully that she had stood first. *(Indirect)*
   Della said, "Hurrah ! I have stood first." *(Direct)*

3. The general called the soldier a coward angrily and ordered him to be off. *(Indirect)*
   The general said to the soldier, "You coward ! be off." *(Direct)*

4. Angelina wished Alice good morning and asked her how she was. *(Indirect)*
   Angelina said, "Good morning, Alice ! how are you ?" *(Direct)*

5. The master rebuked his servant calling him a fool. *(Indirect)*
   The master said to his servant, "You fool ! why have you disturbed me?" *(Direct)*

6. The general praised his brave soldiers exclaiming that they had carried the day. *(Indirect)*
   The general said, "Bravo ! you have carried the day, my brave soldiers." *(Direct)*

7. The young actress exclaimed sorrowfully that she had become a widow. *(Indirect)*
   The young actress said, "Ah me ! I have become a widow." *(Direct)*

8. The master exclaimed regretfully that he had been very silly. *(Indirect)*
   The master said, "Ah ! how silly I have been !" *(Direct)*

TEST YOURSELF

A. Change each sentence to its *indirect speech* :

1. The rich man said, "Alas ! I am undone."
   ....

2. The failed student said, "If only I had worked hard !"
   ....

3. The host said to the guests, "Good-bye, friends ! we had a jolly good time here."
   ....

4. The spectators said, "Well done ! a really good shot."
   ....

5. The pupils said to the teacher, "Good morning, sir !"
   ....
6. The crow said, "How foolish I have been indeed !"
   ....
7. The queen said, "What a charming scenery !"
   ....
8. The host said, "Welcome, my friend ! share my humble food."
   ....
9. The accused said, "By heavens ! I am innocent."
   ....
10. The boy said, "Oh ! How clever I am."
    ....

B. Change each sentence to its *direct form* :
1. The tourist exclaimed in surprise that the sight was really wonderful.
   ....
2. The dying soldier bade good-bye to his dear motherland.
   ....
3. The father rebuked his son for saying something nonsense.
   ....
4. The animals exclaimed in approval that it was really a wonderful plan.
   ....
5. The chairman exclaimed in wonder that it was a very melodious song.
   ....
6. The shopkeeper confessed that he had been very silly.
   ....
7. The doctor exclaimed hatefully that the baby was very dirty.
   ....
8. The athlete exclaimed in joy that he had won the race.
   ....

9. My father called me a fool and asked me in anger why I had wasted the money in gambling.

　　　..

　　　..

10. The sister said to her younger brother why he was pulling her hair like that.

　　　..

C. Change the *form of speech* :

1. The master felt sorry and confessed that he had been mistaken.

　　　..

2. The boy said, "Dad ! you are great indeed."

　　　..

3. The host said to the guests, "Good-bye, my friends !"

　　　..

4. The fox said proudly that he had very cleverly cheated the crow.

　　　..

5. The rich man said, "My God ! I am ruined."

　　　..

6. The failed student exclaimed regretfully that he had not worked hard for the test.

　　　..

7. The students stood up and wished their teacher good morning.

　　　..

8. "You fool ! why have you plucked this flower ?" said the gardener.

　　　..

9. The host said to the guest, "Welcome, my friend ! come in and have a seat."

　　　..

10. The officer rebuked the clerk, "So many mistakes in a single page ?"

　　　..

14 SPEECH—DIRECT AND INDIRECT—VI

We have learnt how to change all the five chief kinds of sentences from Direct to Indirect form of Speech and vice versa. In this lesson we shall study **how to change some typical types** of sentences from one form of speech to another.

CONVERSION OF TYPICAL SENTENCES

Observe the following examples :

A. FROM DIRECT TO INDIRECT

1. The servant said to his master, "Lots of thanks, sir, for your timely help." *(Direct)*
   The servant thanked his master a lot for his timely help. *(Indirect)*

2. The peon said, "I haven't stolen the watch." *(Direct)*
   The peon denied having stolen the watch. *(Indirect)*

3. The accused said, "By Heavens ! I am innocent." *(Direct)*
   The accused exclaimed on oath that he was innocent. *(Indirect)*

4. The master said, "No doubt ! I am in the wrong." *(Direct)*
   The master confessed openly that he was in the wrong. *(Indirect)*

5. The worker said to the officer, "Rest assured, sir ; I shall complete the job in time. *(Direct)*
   The worker assured the officer that he would complete the job in time *(Indirect)*

6. The king said to the rebels, "You traitors ! you will be put to death before long." *(Direct)*
   The king called the rebels traitors and threatened them that they would be put to death before long. *(Indirect)*

7. The accused said to the judge, "God knows, My Lord ; I never abused her." *(Direct)*
   The accused called upon God to witness and told the judge that he had never abused her. *(Indirect)*

8. The pupil said to the teacher, "May I come in, sir ?" *(Direct)*
   The pupil asked for the teacher's permission to go in. *(Indirect)*

9. I said to the officer, "Words fail me to thank you, sir." *(Direct)*
   I expressed my feeling saying that words failed me to thank the officer. *(Indirect)*

B. INDIRECT TO DIRECT

1. The officer enquired of me on oath whether I was to blame (Indirect) or not.
   The officer said to me, "Tell me on oath you are to blame or not" (Direct)
2. She called upon God to witness that she would never (Indirect) repeat the mistake in life.
   She said, "God knows ; I'll never repeat this mistake in life." (Direct)
3. The candidate respectfully asked for the chairman's (Indirect) permission to take a seat.
   The candidate said to the chairman, "Am I allowed to (Direct) take a seat, sir ?
4. Misty exclaimed in wonder to see Erika there. (Indirect)
   Misty said, "Hello Erika ! What a surprise to see you here ?" (Direct)
5. The servant confessed his fault and asked for his (Indirect) master's pardon.
   The servant said, "I am at fault, sir. Pardon me for what I did." (Direct)
6. The rich man exclaimed for help shouting Thief, Thief (Indirect) and urged the people to catch him.
   The rich man said, "Thief ! Thief !! catch him." (Direct)

TEST YOURSELF

A. Change each sentence to its *indirect form* :

1. James said to me, "Hello ! how are you here ?"
   ....
2. The stranger said to me, "Thanks for the cup of tea."
   ....
3. The thief said to the judge, "Upon my honour ! I am quite innocent."
   ....
4. The king said to the clown, "You wretch ! you will be punished for your rudeness."
   ....
   ....

5. The shopkeeper said to the customer, "You rascal ! why have you come here again ?"
   ....
   ....

6. The master said to his servant, "What ! you are still here."
   ....

7. The daughter said to her mother, "Rest assured, mom; I won't let any trouble come to you."
   ....
   ....

8. The maid said to herself, "I have been silly indeed."
   ....

9. The money-lender said to the queen, "By God ! I am not to blame."
   ....

10. The father said to his spoilt son, "Why don't you die of shame ?"
    ....

B. Change each sentence to its *direct form* :

1. The teacher cried out shame on those who copied in the test.
   ....

2. The maid denied having stolen the necklace.
   ....

3. The thief pleaded guilty and asked for the judge's pardon.
   ....

4. The farmer condemned the jackal calling it a thief and threatened it that he would hang it to death.
   ....
   ....

5. The examinee entreated the supervisor to allow him to go to the toilet.
   ....

6. The accused thanked the king again and again for sparing his life.
   ....

7. The policeman hailed the stranger in a rough tone and asked him why he was roaming there.
   ....
   ....

8. Lucy wished Eddie good morning and asked him how he was.
   ....

DIALOGUES

When a dialogue is changed into reported speech, it takes the shape of a passage. Remember that while doing this, great care is taken in connecting the sentences. *Observe the following examples* :

1. DIRECT SPEECH

Betsy : Mac, will you be going home on Christmas day ?"
Mac : "Yes, I will."
Betsy : "Will you please take me down in your car and drop me home ?"
Mac : "Sure, it will be a pleasure for me indeed."
Betsy : Thanks a lot, Mac. How good of you indeed !"
Mac : No mention, please.

INDIRECT SPEECH

Betsy asked Mac whether he would be going home on Christmas day and Mac replied that he would. Then Betsy requested him to take her down in his car and drop her home. Mac assured her that he would do that gladly and Betsy thanked him and applauded him saying that it was so good on his part. Mac replied in a mannerly way that she need not have mentioned that.

2. DIRECT SPEECH

Police Officer : "Who are you and where have you come from ?"
Stranger : "I am Clark and I have come from New York. But why are you asking me that, sir ?"
Police Officer : "I am a police and I am here to inspect strangers. I have come to know that a thief is active in the market."
Stranger : "But I am not that bad fellow, sir."
Police Officer : "Can't you be his companion ?"
Stranger : "Do I look a person likely to keep company with thieves, sir ?"
Constable : Sorry, my boy ; I am really sorry to have suspected you.

INDIRECT SPEECH

The Police Officer asked the stranger who he was and where he had come from. The stranger replied that he was Clark and that he had come there from New York. He further demanded why he was being asked that. The Police Officer told him that he was a police and was there to inspect strangers. He added that he had come

TEST YOURSELF

to know that a thief was active in the market. Clark assured the officer that he was not the thief. But the officer retorted that he could be the companion of the thief. At this Clark enquired respectfully if he looked a person likely to keep company with thieves. The officer had no answer to give and so he felt extremely sorry to have suspected him.

Rewrite the following dialogues in continuous passages as reported speech :

Mark	:	Hello David ! Do you know that the school trip to Malaysia has been cancelled ?
David	:	No, I didn't know that. Why has the trip been cancelled ?
Mark	:	Our school principal is a little worried about our safety.
David	:	Why is she worried ?
Mark	:	It has been raining heavily during the past four weeks. Our principal feels that it is not safe for the children to go during this time.

....

....

....

....

Mother	:	Who do you think will win the match ?
Daughter	:	Who is wearing blue ?
Mother	:	New Zealand.
Daughter	:	Who are the men in yellow ?
Mother	:	They are the Australians.
Daughter	:	They will surely win the match.
Mother	:	Oh ! Why do you feel so ?
Daughter	:	There are 11 of them against just two New Zealanders .

....

....

....

....

15 PUNCTUATION—I

The word—**punctutation**—means the *act of interrupting at intervals*. In grammar, **punctuation** means *the use of certain marks in writing and printing in order to make the writing clearer in its meaning.*

The marks used for punctuation are called **punctuation marks**. There are twelve punctuation marks in all.

1. The Full Stop or Period (.) 2. The Question Mark (?)
3. The Exclamation Mark (!) 4. The Comma (,)
5. Quotation Marks (" ") 6. The Colon (:)
7. The Semi Colon (;) 8. The Dash (—)
9. The Hyphen (-) 10. The Apostrophe (')
11. Parentheses ( ) 12. Brackets [ ]

Let us read about these punctuation marks one by one in detail.

1. THE FULL STOP OR PERIOD

This punctuation mark stands for the longest pause. It is used as under :

A. **At the end of** *assertive sentences (statements)* ; as—
   1. The sun rises in the east.
   2. The boys made a noise.

B. **At the end of** *imperative sentences* ; as—
   1. Be kind to the poor and the needy.
   2. Get out of my sight, at once.
   3. Please help me out of this trouble.
   4. Let us learn from our mistakes.

C. **With some** *abbreviations* ; as—
   1. Feb. = February 2. Lt. = Lieutenant
   3. M.D. = Managing Director 4. Co. = Company

☞ **REMEMBER:**
   1. In direct speech, we put the full stop at the end of a sentence inside the inverted commas.

113

2. Roman Numerals—I, V etc.—are not followed by full stops.
3. Page numbers in books are also not followed by full stops.
4. Numbers used in lists and outlines are followed by full stops.
5. Code words—FBI, SOS, WHO, UNO—are not followed by full stops.

2. THE QUESTION MARK

This mark is used at the end of *questions, i.e. interrogative sentences*. It is also called the **mark of interrogation**. It is used as under :

- A. **At the end of a *direct question* beginning with a helping verb :**
  1. Do you understand this rule clearly ?
  2. Have you had your lunch or not ?
- B. **At the end of a *direct question* beginning with a question word :**
  1. What makes you laugh so loudly ?
  2. Where do you hail from ?

REMEMBER :

We never use a *question mark* at the end of an **indirect question**. It is followed by a full stop ; as—

1. I know who has done it.
2. Let me know what you want.

3. EXCLAMATION MARK

This mark follows *interjection words, vocatives, optative sentences* and *exclamatory sentences* ; as—

- A. **After Interjections :**

  Hurrah !   Aha !   Ah me !   Pooh !

- B. **After Vocatives :**
  1. Help me out of this trouble, O God !
  2. Father ! should I stay on or leave my place ?
  3. Daniel ! where are you, my brother ?
- C. **At the end of Optative Sentences :**
  1. May you live a long happy life !
  2. May God bless you with all His gifts !
  3. May you be doomed, O tyrant !

D.   At the end of Exclamatory Sentences :
1.   How cold it is !
2.   If only I were a prince !
3.   Listen all of you present here !
4.   Well done, my brave soldiers !

REMEMBER :
1.   The sentence that follows the exclamation mark put after an interjection, **starts with a small letter**, not with a capital one.
2.   But the sentence that follows an exclamatory sentence, starts with a **capital letter.**

TEST YOURSELF

A. Answer the following questions :

1.   Which two types of sentences end with full stops ?
     ....

2.   After which four types of words and sentences are exclamation marks used ?
     ....
     ....

3.   What does a *direct question* have at its end ? Give one example.
     ....
     Example : ....

4.   What does an *indirect question* have at its end ? Give one example.
     ....
     Example : ....

B.   **Punctuate the following sentences with** *full stops, questions marks* **and** *exclamation marks.* **Also** *capitalise* **the necessary words:**

1.   at last we reached the city of paris
     ....

2.   the teacher asked stella why she was crying
     ....

3. i've got to buy shoes and jeans
   ....

4. has he arrived at his office
   ....

5. let me know where he lives
   ....

6. let us enjoy swing-rides in the park
   ....

7. may our soldiers be victorious at the field
   ....

8. she is a student of mathematics
   ....

9. hello how are you here
   ....

10. I know where my boss lives
    ....

11. may you be doomed right now
    ....

12. how lovely is the rose
    ....

13. how lovely the rose is
    ....

14. lions tigers panthers and leopards belong to the cat family
    ....

15. he was honest sincere hardworking and faithful
    ....

16. we must never cheat anyone
    ....

17. let us go boating in the canal
    ....

4. THE COMMA

The comma is the most commonly used punctuation mark as it is used in more ways than any other mark. Given below are the ways in which it is used :

A. **It is used to separate *words* and *phrases* in series ; as—**
   1. Sea-food consists of fish, crabs, shrimps and lobsters.
   2. The continent Asia consists of countries like China, Japan, Korea and Thailand.
B. **It is used after *dates* and in *addresses* ; as—**
   1. On March 19, 1949.   2. July 5, 1965.
   2. 668/4, Victoria Street, London
   3. T/128, Church Street, Paris
C. **It is used *after* or *before* a vocative ; as—**
   1. Ladies and gentlemen, listen to me.
   2. Where are you, Dear Mother ?
D. **It is used *before direct quotations* ; as—**
   1. He said to me, "You are the dearest of all to me."
   2. The teacher said, "Why don't you improve your handwriting?"
E. **It is used after the words—*yes*, *no*—in answers ; as—**
   1. Yes, I came to see you yesterday also.
   2. No, he will never accept the condition.
F. **It is used to mark off certain words—*now*, *however*, *for instance*— When any of them marks a break in expression ; as—**
   1. However, try to borrow money without interest.
   2. Rats, for instance, are rodents since they nibble food.
G. **It separates *short co-ordinate clauses* ; as—**
   1. The victor came, he conquered and he went back.
   2. I rose, had my bath, took tea and left the house.
H. **It separates *sub-ordinates clauses* ; as—**
   1. I shall help you, if you return my money.
   2. We stood horrified, but God sent help for us.
I. **It is used after the word—*well*—used as an interjection ; as—**
   1. Well, come in and let me know what you want.
   2. Well, that is right but I am helpless in this matter.
J. **It is used to *separate two qualifications* ; as—**
   1. M.A., B.Ed.   2. M.A., M. Phil   3. M.A., Ph. D.

K. **It is used after *salutations* and *endings* in letters ; as—**
   1. Dear Uncle,   2. Dear Fred,   3. My Dear Mother,
      Yours obediently,   Yours sincerely,   Yours faithfully,

L. **It is used to mark off *the repetition* of a word for stress ; as—**
   1. The fox is a very, very cunning animal.
   2. The rich man shouted "Thief, Thief."

M. **It is used to mark off *titles* and *nicknames* ; as—**
   1. Alexander, the Great, was a powerful emperor.
   2. Eric, the Red, was called so because he had red hair.

TEST YOURSELF

Put *commas* where necessary :

1. Our soldiers are brave courageous and tough.
   ....

2. Gary always helps his friends and class-fellows.
   ....

3. Here is your pen my friend.
   ....

4. Our cricketers will play in Australia, England, New Zealand and Sydney.
   ....

5. *Shakespeare said "Brevity is the soul of wit."*
   ....

6. Alfred my son has topped the list of successful candidates.
   ....

7. Try try till you are successful.
   ....

8. What is then your final decision ?
   ....

9. Yes you are perfectly right.
   ....

10. Matthew M.A. B.Ed.
    ....

11. He came he fought he conquered.
    ....

12. Well we are certainly mistaken.
    ....

13. Napolean the poltical leader was a brave general.
    ....

14. Come forward and touch him if you dare.
    ....

15. We can however do something for you.
    ....

16. Our test will start on March 16 2008.
    ....

17. The baby who was fast asleep suddenly gave out a cry.
    ....

18. Only a few days before she reached here from London.
    ....

19. My office is at 668/4 Street Number 2 New York City USA
    ....

5. QUOTATION MARKS

Quotation marks or *inverted commas* or raised commas are used as under:

A. **To enclose** *directly reported speeches* ; as—
   1. Cindrella said, " I am going to the market."
   2. "Beauty needs no ornament," is a popular saying.

B. **To enclose titles of** *objects, written items* **or** *books* ; as—
1. "Julius Caesar" is the work of Shakespeare, not of Woodsworth.
2. The sailors sailed in the "Victory" to England.

6. THE COLON

This punctuation mark is used as under :
A. **To introduce** *sayings* ; as—
1. They say : Brevity is the soul of wit.
2. It is said : Truth conquers in the long run.
B. **It is used after the expression like** *as follows* ; as—
1. Chief rivers of North-America are :
    (a) Mississippi   (b) The Ohio
    (c) The Yukon

7. THE SEMI COLON

The semicolon is a longer pause than a comma. It is used as under :
A. **It is used** *between two clauses of a compound sentence* ; as—
1. To err is human ; to forgive, divine.
2. The powerful are often cruel ; the weak, kind.
B. **It is used** *between clauses of a compound sentence* **even if a conjunction is there and if the clauses contain commas** ; as—
1. We marched on staggering, murmuring and cursing our lot ; but ultimately reached our destination.
2. I have no funds ; so I can't buy a new suit.
C. **It is used to** *separate groups* **separated by commas** ; as—
1. mete, meet, meat ; by, buy, bye ; fair, fare
D. When examples are introduced by using *e.g.* or *viz.*, they are preceded by a **semicolon** ; as—
1. There are five qualities of a student ; *viz.*, *devotion, honesty, character, attention* and *short sleep*.
2. Good correspondence has three qualities ; *e.g. politeness, promptness and precision*.

TEST YOURSELF

A. Rewrite using *quotation marks*, *colons* and *semicolons* where necessary :

1. I am unwell therefore I won't go to school today.
   ....

2. Everybody needs air to breathe water to drink and food to eat.
   ....

3. Distinguish between the following word-pairs :

   sale, sail   here, hear   boy, buoy   so, sow
   ....

4. Chief rivers of South-America are the Mississippi, the Ohio, and the Yukon.
   ....

5. The son said what can I do for you, dad ?
   ....

6. Truth is another name for God, they say.
   ....

7. Lyrics are of another types the ode, the elegy, the sonnet and the song.
   ....

8. To my seniors I am obedient to my juniors I am loving.
   ....

9. As Caesar loved me I wept for him as he was fortunate I honour him but as he was ambitious I slew him.
   ....

10. It should be our motto if anyone should not work, he/she should not eat as well.
    ....

16 PUNCTUATION—II

1. **DASH**

   It is used as under :

   A. **After the colon** (*though rarely now*) ; as—

   The results of this policy were as under :

   1. ....
   2. ....
   3. ....

   B. **To mark a *parenthetic part* in a sentence** ; as—

   1. At last—to cut a long story short—we reached our destination.
   2. She is—to tell you the truth—a shop-lifter.
   3. You are—if I am not in the wrong—Gilbert.

   C. **To sum up a number of items** ; as—

   1. Efficiency, management, satisfaction among workers—these are necessary for a good business.
   2. Money, honour, family—these have no value for a dying person.
   3. Apples, mangoes, oranges, grapes—all these are very good for health.

   D. **To mark off a sudden *change of thought*** ; as—

   1. Coming to the next point—I fear, I am boring you.
   2. If you want to sell your watch—by the way, have you got its receipt of purchase ?
   3. I am looking for Chris—may I know who you are ?

   E. **Before a *repeated word*** ; as—

   1. Tendencies to lying to stealing, to teasing—so common among children—need to be curbed through examples.

2. **HYPHEN**

   Hyphen is used as under :

   A. To form compound words ; **as—**

   brother-in-law   book-worm   touch-me-not

   up-to-date   hide-and-seek

B. To divide words into syllables ; as—

pa-ra-graph	un-cer-tain	but-ter-cup
sa-tis-fy	busi-ness	effi-ciency

TEST YOURSELF

A. Punctuate each sentence using a *dash* or a *hyphen* where necessary:

1. Health, wealth and character all these are necessary for a happy and full life.
   ....

2. Our class room has two doors and four windows.
   ....

3. If only I had been intelligent but why cry over spilt milk.
   ....

4. The old man died as he had lived long without any illness.
   ....

5. At last to be brief the ship reached the harbour.
   ....

6. My health, wealth, peace of mind all these were lost only due to my immense greed.
   ....

7. God must be kind to us yes surely.
   ....

8. I went to see my father in law in the hospital as he was under going treatment there.

B. Here are two columns A,B of ten words each. Take one word from A and one from B to make *a compound word* using hyphen :

	A	B	
1.	month	hearted	....

123

2.	side	ache	....
3.	kind	note	....
4.	shoe	out	....
5.	step	nots	....
6.	class	track	....
7.	foot	son	....
8.	tooth	room	....
9.	have	end	....
10.	hide	shine	....

C. Given below are three columns A, B, C of eight words. Take one word from each column and form *a compound word* using two hyphens :

	A	B	C	
1.	father	and	interview	....
2.	touch	of	war	....
3.	forget	for	nothing	....
4.	tug	in	law	....
5.	hide	me	not	....
6.	good	in	chief	....
7.	Editor	in	seek	....
8.	walk	me	not	....

3. THE APOSTROPHE

This mark is used as under :

A. to indicate the omission of some letter or letters ; as—
don't ;   e'er ;   o'er ;   it's

B. To mark the possessive case ; as—
student's dress ;   children's song

C. To make plurals of letters or figures ; as—
5's ;   t's ;   B.A.'s

Remember the following short forms of some common words. These words involve the use of apostrophe and are called **clipped forms** or **contractions**.

Word	Contraction	Word	Contraction
I am	I'm	had not	hadn't

I shall/will	I'll	cannot	can't
I have	I've	could not	couldn't
He has/is	He's	should not	shouldn't
You are	You're	would not	wouldn't
do not	don't	might not	mightn't
does not	doesn't	ought not	oughtn't
did not	didn't	must not	mustn't
shall not	shan't	it is	It's
will not	won't	ever	e'er
is not	isn't	never	ne'er
are not	aren't	over	o'er
was not	wasn't	even	e'en
were not	weren't	honourable	hon'ble
have not	haven't		
has not	hasn't		

4. PARENTHESES ( )

These marks mark off the part/parts of a sentence than can be easily omitted. These parts are not related to the rest of the sentence grammatically.

1. I have already told you (you don't remember perhaps) why I cannot accompany you to Singapore.

5. BRACKETS [ ]

These marks, enclose explanations and directions that are not a part of the actual speech.

"I am a simple person." [Laughter]

The minister [seriously] said that he wanted to retire due to ill health.

TEST YOURSELF

A. Put the mark *of apostrophe* where needed :

1. Alfred wife was named Betsy.

2. Shakespeares King Lear is a tragic play.
   ....

3. Do not forget to dot your *is* and cross your *ts*.
   ....

4. What is the sum if we add up four 5s together ?
   ....

5. It is not a childs play to perform such a trick.
   ....

6. He has done yeomans service to the nation.
   ....

7. The danger is looming large like the Damocles sword.
   ....

8. I do not like your habit of *ifs* and *buts*.
   ....

9. A wise person considers the hows and whys of things before doing it.
   ....

10. Even BAs and MAs are roaming without jobs these days.
    ....

11. Too much snubbing spoils a childs future.
    ....

B. Insert *parentheses* in each sentence where necessary :

1. What can I do you have no sense of shame to make you a man in the real sense.
2. How many times should I tell you are so forgetful that we cannot accept these terms.

C. Insert *brackets* in each sentence where necessary :

1. Hang the man around whose neck the noose fits. Laughter
2. The queen in her mind thought of poisoning the king.

SOLVED EXAMPLES ON PUNCTUATION

1. the guest entered the room went up to the host and shook hands with him.   *(Unpunctuated)*

The guest entered the room, went up to the host and
shook hands with him.   *(Punctuated)*

2. we'll go to Paris to see the Eiffel Tower said they.   *(Unpunctuated)*

    "We'll go to Paris to see the Eiffel Tower," said they.   *(Punctuated)*

3. many were called for interview but few seleected.   *(Unpunctuated)*

    Many were called for interview ; but few, selected.   *(Punctuated)*

4. my goodness what should I do now.   *(Unpunctuated)*

    My Goodness ! what should I do now ?   *(Punctuated)*

5. true muslims regard the holy quran their most sacred book and they say their prayer (*namaz*) five times a day, said the priest.   *(Unpunctuated)*

    "True Muslims regard the Holy Quran their most sacred book and they say their prayer (namaz) five times a day," said the priest. *(Punctuated)*

6. I have a severe headache sir may I go home said the student why did you come to school if you were unwell.   *(Unpunctuated)*

    "I have a severe headache, sir. May I go home," said the student. "Why did you come to school if you were unwell ?" said the teacher.

TEST YOURSELF

A. Punctuate the following :

1. may I come in sir

    ....

2. help me out of this trouble o god

    ....

3. I like grapes mangoes oranges and apples. all these are good for health what do you like by the way said alex to his friend leonard

    ....

    ....

    ....

4. rest assured dad I must achieve a distinction said the son

    ....

127

5. jessica you are not at fault
   ....

6. don't worry mother you ll be all right soon said the son
   ....

7. whenever I approached a peasant's house towards night-fall I played one of the most merry tunes
   ....
   ....

B. Punctuate each paragraph :

1. for what deed o god are you punishing me like this bewailed the widow don t curse your lot my dear daughter everything will be all right before long said her father
   ....
   ....
   ....

2. soon we got to a fruit-seller shop who smiled a welcome saying really five apples for five cents sir
   ....
   ....

3. who is the man in the fortune my son said the old father he is vasco da gama papa who was he and what did he do asked the old man he was a famous sailor who discovered a sea-route to India said the son
   ....
   ....
   ....
   ....
   ....

17 ANALYSIS OF SENTENCES

ANALYSIS OF COMPLEX SENTENCES

A *complex sentence* is a sentence made up of a *main clause* and one or more *dependent clauses*.

A. THE MAIN CLAUSE

The *main clause* of a complex sentence is the clause that contains *the main verb* of the entire complex sentence.

B. THE DEPENDENT CLAUSE

A *dependent clause* is a clause that depends on the main clause and as a whole does the work of a *noun*, an *adjective* or an *adverb*.

Clearly, there are three kinds of dependent clauses :

1. The Noun Clause 2. The Adjective Clause 3. The Adverb Clause

1. THE NOUN CLAUSE

    A *noun clause* is a dependent or sub-ordinate clause that does the work of a *noun* in relation to the main clause or some word in it.

2. THE ADJECTIVE CLAUSE

    An *adjective clause* is a dependent clause that does the work of an *adjective* in relation to the main clause or some word in it.

3. THE ADVERB CLAUSE

    An *adverb clause* is a dependent clause that does the work of an *adverb* in relation to the main clause or some word in it.

THE NOUN CLAUSE

A. A noun clause *is introduced by using three types of connectives*:

(a) conjunction—**that**   (b) a question word—**when, which,** etc.

(c) a relating word—**who, whose,** etc.

Examples :
1. I did not know **that** he would cheat us in this way.
2. **Where** he comes from is not known to me.
3. Ask her **whether** she will accompany us or not.

B. **A noun clause** *can be*—

(a) **subject** *to a verb* :
1. *Where he came from* **was** not known to me.
2. *That he will help us* **is** quite certain.
3. *Whether he insulted them* **is** doubtful.

(b) **Object** *to a verb* :
1. I want to **know** *where you come from*.
2. He has **promised** me that *he would soon be back*.
3. **Realizing** *what crime he had done*, he begged for mercy.

(c) **Object** *to a preposition* :
1. *His* success depends **on** *how hard he works*.
2. You will have to pay **for** *what you buy*.
3. **Except** that *he is short-tempered*, he is a noble person.

(d) **Complement** *to a verb* :
1. That **is** *what I expected from her*.
2. The point **was** *whether we should go further or not*.
3. The result **will be** *what we want it to be*.

(e) In **apposition** *to a noun* :
1. The report *that some taxes have been removed* is pleasing.
2. The rumour *that she is not coming today* is false.
3. The fact *that the earth is round* is by all means correct.

TEST YOURSELF

Pick out the *noun clause* in each sentence and mention its function :

1. It appears that my orders have been carried out.
   N. Cl. .... Function ....
2. He sent out an order that trouble-makers should be punished.
   N. Cl .... Function ....
3. Nobody could understand why the plan had failed.
   N. Cl. .... Function ....

4. That she was also to blame could not be proved.
   N. Cl. .... Function ....
5. The main point is when we shall be free from debt.
   N. Cl. .... Function ....
6. The sense that he is all alone has got over his mind.
   N. Cl. ....Function ....
7. History tells us how the region was invaded again and again.
   N. Cl. .... Function ....
8. New York is quite far off from Paris is a hard fact.
   N. Cl. .... Function ....
9. How it came to happen is not known to anyone.
   N. Cl. .... Function ....
10. We must know that active children are never at rest.
    N. Cl. .... Function ....
11. Know *Thyself*—was the advice given to us by a wise man.
    N. Cl. .... Function ....

THE ADJECTIVE CLAUSE

The Adjective Clause does the work of an adjective on the whole. It can be introduced using *connectives* that are either **pronouns** or **adverbs**.

Observe the following examples :

1. I called on your mother **who** was pleased to see me.
2. I called at his house **where** I was welcomed warmly.

TEST YOURSELF

Pick out the *adjective clause* in each sentence and mention the *noun* which it qualifies :

1. There are instruments that help us to see heavenly bodies.
   Adj. Cl. .... Noun ....
2. The thief who commited the theft has been arrested.
   Adj. Cl. .... Noun ....

3. All that glitters is not gold.
   Adj.. Cl...................................... *Noun* ....

4. Of what use is the knowledge that fails to create virtue.
   Adj.. Cl...................................... *Noun* ....

5. The plan we had thought of worked very well.
   Adj.. Cl...................................... *Noun* ....

6. The story that you are telling is certainly untrue.
   Adj.. Cl...................................... *Noun* ....

7. Such men as who are dishonest are never respected.
   Adj.. Cl...................................... *Noun* ....

8. I cannot tell you the time when I am to return.
   Adj.. Cl...................................... *Noun* ....

9. I have seen the house where Thomas lived.
   Adj.. Cl...................................... *Noun* ....

THE ADVERB CLAUSE

The *Adverb Clause* **does the work of an** *adverb* **to some** *verb, adjective* **or in the main clause :**

Adverb clauses are introduced using **conjunctions** of *time, manner, contrast, comparison condition, purpose, reason, effect,* etc.

Observe the following examples :

1. *He will pass the test* **since** *he has worked very hard.*   (*reason*)
2. *He worked very hard* **so** *he passed the test.*   (*result/effect*)
3. *He worked hard* **so that** *he might pass the test.*   (*purpose*)
4. *I shall pass the test* **if** *I work hard.*   (*condition*)
5. *I passed the test* **though** *I had not worked hard.*   (*contrast*)
6. *I got marks more* **than** *he obtained in the test.*   (*comparison*)
7. *I will get marks* **just** *as I work hard.*   (*manner*)
8. *I shall pass the tests* **as long as** *I work hard.*   (*time*)

TEST YOURSELF

Pick the *adverb clause* and mention its *function* :

1. She must succeed because she has worked very hard.
   Adv. Cl. .... Function ....
2. Men go out for work so that they may earn money.
   Adv. Cl. .... Function ....
3. I did not confess though they beat me severely.
   Adv. Cl. .... Function ....
4. I like you as much as anybody else does.
   Adv. Cl. .... Function ....
5. Walk carefully lest you should stumble.
   Adv. Cl. .... Function ....
6. Learn to deserve before you desire.
   Adv. Cl. .... Function ....
7. The mice will play when the cat is away.
   Adv. Cl. .... Function ....
8. He exercised so much patience that he succeeded at last.
   Adv. Cl. .... Function ....
9. By sunset I must reach where my elder brother lives.
   Adv. Cl. .... Function ....

REVISIONAL EXERCISES

Analyse each sentence giving the name of the *clause* along with its *function* :

1. When I returned from Los Angeles, I found she had recovered from the shock which was the result of unpleasant events.
2. He backed away from me as if I were an animal or a robber with a weapon.
3. When he had got near the door, he glowered at me in anger.
4. He knew well that it would be impossible to find such a book in Germany.
5. With earnest feelings shall I pray,
   For thee when I'm far away ;

For never have I seen a grace,

Which is there on your charming face.

6. That he has agreed to protect our rights is really admirable.
7. The tree is so high that a crow sitting on its top seems cawing in another region.
8. The years that followed Clive's return to England, saw the government of the Company go down to such a point as cannot be believed.
9. One evening I was visited by a tall young lady whose charms cast a spell on me.
10. As soon as we got ready to take a photograph, someone came and asked us whether we knew that we were doing a wrong thing.
11. We apologised and explained that because we could find nobody about, we were going to take a snap of the monument.
12. As it is necessary that the reader must know something about the young boy who will appear in the following pages of the play, I'll state who and what he was.
13. Blessed is the man who keeps away from the wicked.
14. Nothing can describe the confusion at thought which I had when I was about to be drowned.
15. In his seventieth year, the king had a fall which broke his arm and leg.
16. The root coming out of the seed strikes into the ground and when it has got fixed in the earth, the sap that was flowing downwards begins to flow upwards.
17. They hoped that the king would either treat the matter as a joke or punish

ANALYSIS OF COMPOUND SENTENCES

A *compound sentence* is a sentence made up of two or more simple sentences joined together using co-ordinate *conjunction* ; as—

1. The sun rose **and** the fog disappeared.
2. He came to see me **but** I was not at home.
3. We reached home tired, **for** we had walked all day.

As a compound sentence is made up of simple sentences, its analysis is just like the analysis of simple sentence. Only the **conjunction** joining those sentences has to be shown separate. Let us have *a few examples*.

The sentences below has two simple sentences joined by **and, but, for**.

1. The sun rose.   and   The fog disappeared.
2. He came to see me.   but   I was not at home.
3. We reached home tired   for   We had walked all day.

No.	Connective	Subject	Enlargement of Subject	verb	Object	Enlargement of object	Complement	Adverbials
1.	and	1. sun 2. fog	The the	rose disappeared	-- --	-- --	-- --	
2.	but	1. He 2. I	-- --	came was	-- --	-- --	to see me not at home	-- --
3.	for	1. We 2. We	-- --	reached had walked	home --	-- --	-- --	tired all day

TEST YOURSELF

Analyse the following *compound sentences* :

1. The boy ran away and the old man was left alone.
   ....
2. Rachel went home and dropped herself on the bed.
   ....
3. She did her duty and struck to her post even in danger.
   ....
4. We did not like towns and always live in the countryside.
   ....
5. She was deeply worried but pretended to be asleep.
   ....

18 SYNTHESIS OF SENTENCES

WHAT IS SYNTHESIS ?

Synthesis **is the process of just opposite to** *analysis.* **In other words,** *it is the process of building the clauses together.*

The process can be dealt with under three headings as under :

1. **COMBINING TWO OR MORE SIMPLE SENTENCES INTO A SINGLE SIMPLE SENTENCE**

   These sentences are combined in the following six ways.

   (a) **Using Participles**

   He ran away. He had seen a bear coming.

   Seeing a bear coming, he ran away.

   (b) **Using a Perfect Phrase**

   The sun rose. The fog disappeared.

   The sun **having risen**, the fog disappeared.

   (c) **Using an Infinitive**

   He has got two daughters. He must marry them off.

   He has got two daughters **to marry off**.

   (d) **Using a Phrase in Apposition**

   He fled from the battle-field. It was a cowardly act.

   He fled from the battle-field—**a cowardly act**.

   (e) **Using an Adverb or Adverb Phrase**

   He was committing follies. He was completely unmindful of them.

   He was quite unmindful of his follies.

   (f) **Using a Gerund**

   He advised them usefully. He helped them with money.

   Besides **giving** useful advice, he helped them with money.

TEST YOURSELF

Combine each set of simple sentences into a single *simple sentence*:

A. 1. I sat in a chair. I held my hat in my right hand.
   ....

2. We sat down to rest a while. We had had a tiring journey.
   ....

3. Your letter didn't reach me. It had been addressed wrongly.
   ....

B. 4. The dispute was settled. Everybody felt satisfied.
   ....

5. The fog was very dense. We could not see our way.
   ....

6. The general was killed. The soldiers were filled with fear.
   ....

C. 7. He has a large family. He must support it.
   ....

8. They grow vegetables. They sell them to green-grocers.
   ....

9. There is only one way. By it you can solve this sum.
   ....

D. 10. The moon was bright. We could see our way.
    ....

11. Vasco da Gama found a sea-route to India. It was a milestone in the world history.
    ....

12. Clive came to London as an ordinary clerk. He rose to be the General Manager.
    ....

E. 13. He requested for pardon. The request was rejected.
    ....

14. He will come back to us. He will not be absent for long.
    ....

15. The tree was cut down. It was done gradually.
    ....

F.16. He gave us a promise. He fulfilled it also.
....

17. He is full of sorrow. Still he is hopeful.
....

18. He made a great effort. He achieved his goal.
....

2. COMBINING SIMPLE SENTENCES INTO A COMPOUND SENTENCE

Simple sentences are combined into compound sentences as under :

(a) **Using a Cumulative Conjunction :**
   He was imprisoned. He was fined also.
   He was imprisoned as well as fined.

(b) **Using an Alternative Conjunction :**
   The baby may be a boy. It may be a girl.
   The baby is either a boy or a girl.

(c) **Using an Adversative Conjunction :**
   He is old. He is very active.
   He is old but he is very active.

(d) **Using an Illative Conjunction :**
   Mice fear cats. They run into their holes.
   Mice run into their holes for they fear cats.

TEST YOURSELF

Combine each pair of simple sentences into a *compound sentence*:

1. The monkey weighed the two pieces. He found one to be heavier.
....

2. No one hoped him to pass the test. He passed the test.
....

3. You will have to do it. You will be dismissed otherwise.
....

4. Swimming is a good exercise. Everyone must learn how to swim.
....

5. We came out of the room in time. The roof would have crushed us.
....

6. The plains are very hot in Europe. The hills are cool and pleasant.
....

7. She is a rich lady. She is not proud of her wealth.
....

8. Many were called for interview. Few were selected.
....

9. The sun rose. Darkness disappeared.
....

3. **COMBINING SENTENCES INTO A COMPLEX SENTENCE**

This process is carried out using three types of clauses as under :

A. NOUN CLAUSE

This clause is introduced by using the conjunction that or some relative word ; as—

1. It is certain. The rose is the queen of flowers.
   It is certain **that** the rose is the queen of flowers.
2. He lives at some place. Nobody knows about this place.
   Nobody knows **where** he lives.

TEST YOURSELF

Combine each pair of sentences into a *complex sentence* :

1. She will return in a week. She told me about it.
   ....

2. Someone will come to our help. I am sure of it.
   ....

3. He is innocent. This is the verdict of the court.
   ....

4. How is the patient feeling ? This is my question.
   ....

5. You have passed the examination. It is news to us. We are happy at the news.
   ....

6. A lazy person harms no one but himself or herself. This is a proven fact.
   ....

7. The pasture looks green and pleasant. You can see it with your own eyes.
   ....

8. She advised me. I must make myself known to her.
   ....

9. I believe. This account will be an entertainment to the reader.
   ....

10. I have heard it. The ship foundered and none escaped but the cabin-boy.
    ....

11. He will help us out of this danger. His way of doing so is known to no one.
    ....

12. The field looks green and pleasant. Look at it.
    ....

B. THE ADJECTIVE CLAUSE

When an adjective clause is to be introduced, a *relative pronoun* or *adverb* is used as a **connective** in a *qualifying sense*.

Also remember that the adjective clause must be **quite close** to its noun/pronoun, *i.e.* no word should come in between them ; as—

1. A man had a goose. The goose laid a golden egg daily.
   A man had a *goose* **that** *laid a golden egg daily*.
2. The servant had to perform a duty. The duty was very difficult.
   The servant had to perform *a duty* **which** *was very difficult*.

Combine each pair of simple sentences into a complex sentence :

1. I suffered from worry. The worry was unbearable.
   ....

2. A speaker must have a clear voice. You don't have such voice.
   ....

3. We came upon a village. Only shepherds lived in this village.
   ....

4. A small house stood at the foot-hill. We passed a night there.
   ....

5. The Africans were an ancient nation. The nation was the first to be civilised.
   ....

6. The robbers met secretly at a place. This place was a public park.
   ....

7. Soon we reached a cottage. It had a shady tree by its side.
   ....

8. She received good education. It raised her above other women.
   ....

9. We reached the end of the foot-path. A dead body was lying there.
   ....

10. Androcles came alive out of the den. Lions lived in this den.
    ....

11. He has done me a favour. I cannot repay it in any manner.
    ....

C. THE ADVERB CLAUSE

An adverb clause is introduced using a *sub-ordinating conjunction* or a *relative pronoun* or *adverb* ; as—

1. The fox left off trying any more. He could not reach the grapes.

   The fox left off trying any more **as** he could not reach the grapes.

   (Using a conjunction)

   The fox left off trying any more **when** he couldn't reach the grapes.

   (Using an adverb)

2. My son slept very soundly at night. He must have been very tired.

   My son, **who** slept very soundly at night, must have been very tired.

   (*Using a relative pronoun*)

☞ Remember, **who** = *because he*, in the above sentence.

TEST YOURSELF

Combine each pair of simple sentences into a *complex sentence*.

1. Everyone must die and will be forgotten. Why does then one run after fame?
   ....
2. He got more and more riches. But he never felt satisfied.
   ....
3. A thief goes about his job carefully. He does not want to be caught.
   ....
4. Perry is a lazy boy. No other boy in the class is equally lazy.
   ....
5. He came to realize his folly. He was then very sorry.
   ....
6. He has been very unlucky. He is always cheerful.
   ....
7. Forgive the poor fellow. You are very merciful indeed.
   ....
8. I must get a receipt. Only then shall I pay the money.
   ....
9. Every green plant began to wither. The hot season had set in.
   ....

REVISIONAL EXERCISES

Combine into a single sentence :

1. The murder was proved. The court ordered the culprit to be hanged till death.
   ....

2. You have asked me to visit your house many times. I will not disappoint you any longer.

   ....
   ....

3. She was very disappointed. She left herself to her fate. She refused to take any help.

   ....
   ....

4. He wept bitterly at the sad news. A child would have wept in the same way.

   ....

5. The result may be good or bad. We are now out of danger.

   ....

6. We felt quite carefree. Our worst dangers are over now.

   ....

7. All the ships were in a grave danger. A violent storm was rising.

   ....

8. The lion was let out of the cage. It did not attack the slave. It came to him. It licked his hand. It had recognised him.

   ....
   ....

9. I want you to tell me. How have you done this sum ?

   ....

10. I saw it with my own eyes. I doubted it even then.

    ....

11. He will surely come back. No one knows his time of returning.

    ....

12. I reached Paris. I called on my aunt.

    ....

19 RULES OF AGREEMENT

1 These rules govern the relationship of various parts of a sentence to one another.

A. NOUNS AND PRONOUNS

(a) A **noun** or **pronoun** used predicatively agrees **in case** with the words to which it refers ; as—

1. *He* is a **sailor** of great fame. (*nominative case*)
2. *It* is **he** who killed the cruel giant. (*nominative case*)

(b) A **noun** or **pronoun** that stands in apposition to another **noun or pronoun,** agrees with it **in case** ; as—

1. I met your *brother*, the **architect**. (*objective*)
2. *Mary*, **Queen** of Scots, was imprisoned. (*nominative*)

(c) The pronoun—**It**—is frequently used as an **introductory subject** or **object** having an **infinitive** in apposition ; as—

1. *It* is easy **to do**. (**to do** *is in apposition* **to subject**— *It*)
2. I thought it unwise **to say** such words.
   (**to say** *is in apposition* **to object**— *It*)

(d) A **relative pronoun** agrees in **number** and **person** with its **antecedent** ; as—

1. This is the *man* **who** *wants* to see you.
   (**who** *has the same person, number as* **man**)
2. Punish his son **who** *was* guilty. (**who** *has the same person, number as* **son**)

B. DETERMINERS

The **demonstrative determiners** (*this, that, these, those*) agree in **number** with the **nouns** *that they qualify* ; as—

1. **This** *book*   2. **These** *books*   3. **That** *pen*   4. **Those** *pens*

C. VERBS

A **verb** always agrees with its **subject** in **number** and **person**.

(a) A **double** or **multiple subject** *takes a* **plural verb** ; as—

1. *He* and *I* **are** friends.
2. *You* and *he* **were** there in the park.

(b) The **double subject** expressing the **same idea** has a **singular verb** ; as—
1. The *aim* and *object* of this plan **is** very clear.
2. The sum and substance of his speech has been published.

(c) Two subjects joined by **either.....or/neither....nor** have the verb according to the **latter subject** ; as—
1. Either *he* or *you* **are** to blame.
2. Neither *you* nor *he* **was** to blame.
3. Either *Mac* or *I* **am** to attend the function.
4. Neither *Stella* nor *you* **were** able to do it.

(d) When two subjects are joined by **as well as**, the **verb** is used according to the **first subject** ; as—
1. *We* as well as *he* **are** to complete this job.
2. *He* as well as *we* **is** to complete this job.

(e) When two subjects are joined by **along with**, the verb is used according to the **first subject** ; as—
1. The *king along with his ministers* **was** invited to the function.
2. **All the ministers along with** the *queen* **were** invited to the function.

D. COLLECTIVE NOUNS

(a) **A collective noun** must be treated as **singular** or **plural** consistently in one sentence. ; as—
1. The *council* **has decided** to publish **its** accounts. (*Singular*)
2. The *council* **have** decided to publish **their** accounts. (*Plural*)

(b) **A collective noun** may be regarded **singular** or **plural**. Its verb is also to be used accordingly ; as—

1. A *new committee* **has** been elected.
2. The *committee* **are** divided in their decision.

TEST YOURSELF

A. Point out the *nouns* or *noun-equivalents* used *in apposition* in the sentences given below. Also name the *noun/pronoun* whose apposition is there :

1. Michael, the weaver, is the leader of the gang.

   Phrase in apposition : .... Noun : ....

2. A Mid Summer Night's Dream, a comedy, was written by Shakespeare.
   Phrase in apposition : .... Noun : ....
3. I do not agree with the idea discussed in the meeting.
   Phrase in apposition : .... Noun : ....
4. The theory, that solids are harder than liquids, is quite true.
   Clause in apposition : .... Noun : ....
5. The topic, that a language is a living thing, is very difficult to write on.
   Clause in apposition : .... Noun : ....
6. The steps, under consideration, will be very effective.
   Phrase in apposition : .... Noun : ....

B. Supply a correct *verb* for each blank.
1. The hustle and bustle of the day ....exhausted me.
2. A horse and carriage...................................... at the door.
3. When the police fired, the mob .... seen running in all directions.
4. The committee...................................decided to appoint a cashier.
5. The committee.. of different opinions.
6. It is me who....................... to blame for spoiling the whole game.
7. The teacher as well as the students .... present at the function.
8. Either you or your brother ....at fault.
9. The principal along with the teachers ....honoured by the public.
10. A new government................................. been elected by the people.
11. The jury .... not of one opinion about this matter.
12. The sum and substance of the chairman's speech ....
    there in the report.

C. Supply a *suitable word* for each blank :
1. ....kind of mistake should not be repeated again by you.
2. She and I..................very sincere friends right since our early years.
3. Neither my brother nor I ....to blame for it.
4. That is the man..................................we were looking for.
5. Our aim and object............ to make everything clear to everybody.
6. The committee............................... different views on this subject.
7. They elected............................... their leader for the movement.
8. I thought it unwise to .... such unpleasant news to her.

20 GRAMMATICAL ERRORS

A SUBJECT-VERB AGREEMENT

(a) *Error is caused when* a **plural noun** *comes between* a **singular subject** *and* its verb ; as—

    1. A mountain, broken by ravines, *enclose* this small state. (*incorrect*)
       A mountain, broken by ravines, **encloses** this small state. (*correct*)

(b) *Error occurs when* **two singular subjects** *joined by* **with** *or* **along with** *are given a verb* **according to the latter subject** ; as—

    1. The king with all his ministers *were* murdered. (*incorrect*)
       The king with all his ministers **was** murdered. (*correct*)

(c) *Error occurs when two subjects joined by* **as well as** *are given a verb* **according to the latter subject** ; as—

    1. Mac as well as his friends *were* present there. (*incorrect*)
       Mac as well as his friends **was** present there. (*correct*)

(d) *Error occurs when two singular nouns joined by* **and** *but* **pointing to the same noun** *are given a* **plural verb** ; as—

    1. The king and conqueror *have* arrived. (*incorrect*)
       The king and conqueror *has* arrived. (*correct*)

(e) *Error occurs when two nouns with determiners* **a/an/the** *before them are taken as pointing to the* **same noun** *and* **a singular verb** *is used for them* ; as—

    1. *A black* and *a white cow is* grazing in the pasture. (*incorrect*)
       A black and *a white* **cow are** grazing in the pasture. (*correct*)

    2. *A black and white cow are* grazing in the pasture. (*incorrect*)
       A black and *white* **cow is** grazing in the pasture. (*correct*)

(f) *Error occurs when a* **collective noun** *is treated as* **singular** *in one part and as* **plural** *in another part of the same sentence* ; as—

    1. The crew *was* on board and they got ready to face the storm (*incorrect*)

    2. The crew **were** on board and they got ready to face the storm. (*correct*)

(g) A **noun looking plural** must be followed by a **singular verb** *if it is the name of a singular object*; as—

    1.   Gulliver's Travels *are* the best work of Dean Swift. *(incorrect)*
           Gulliver's Travels **is** the best work of Dean Swift. *(correct)*

    2.   Politics **has** become very dirty these days. *(correct)*

    3.   This news **is** absolutely true. *(correct)*

(h) When a verb has two subjects—*one singular and the other plural—separate verbforms must be used* ; as—

    1.   The stable *has been* broken and the horses stolen. *(incorrect)*
           The stable **has been** broken and the horses **have been** stolen. *(correct)*

(i) **Prepositions** and **transitive verbs** *are followed by objects that are in the* **nominative case** ; as—

    1.   Let *he* and she go together. *(incorrect)*
           Let **him** and **her** go together. *(correct)*

    2.   Between *you* and *I*, it is very likely to happen. *(incorrect)*
           Between **you** and **me**, it is very likely to happen. *(correct)*

    3.   Tell *he* that the sun has risen high. *(incorrect)*
           Tell **him** that the sun has risen high. *(correct)*

    4.   *Who* are you looking for ? *(incorrect)*
           Whom are you looking for ? *(correct)*

(j) A **predicative pronoun** *must agree* **in case** *with the* **word** *it refers to*; as—

    1.   If I were *him*, I should never go. *(incorrect)*
           If I were **he**, I should never go. *(correct)*

(k) **A relative pronoun** *must agree with its* **antecedent** ; as—

    1.   This is one of the events *that has* happened many times. *(incorrect)*
           This is one of the *events* that **have** happened many times. *(correct)*

(l) **Relatives** *must be used correctly in terms of* **case** ; as—

    1.   Mac was a man *whom* we all expected would succeed. *(incorrect)*
           Mac was a man **who** we all expected would succeed. *(correct)*

(m) **Each, every, either, everybody, anybody, nobody, none** *always take* **singular verbs** *or* **pronouns** *or* **adjectives** *after them* ; as—
1. **Each** person who comes there will have **his/her** own views.
2. **Nobody** will be allowed to have **his/her** own way.
3. **Either** of these books **is** very good.
4. **Everything was** in *its* own place.
5. **None** but the brave **deserves** the best.
6. **Every** man **is** to die sooner or later.

(n) **Each other** *and* **either**, *are used for* **two things** *but* **any** *and* **one another** *for* **more than two things**; as—
1. The **two** friends fell out with **each other.**
2. **Either** of the **two** horses is fine.
3. The *three* sons of the farmer fell out with **one another.**
4. Cut **any** of these **four** apples and enjoy it.

(o) **Like** *must never be used as a* **conjunction**. It is improper to say—
1. He does not work *like* his father did. *(incorrect)*

He does not work **as** his father did. *(correct)*

(p) **Than** *should never be used as a* **preposition**. *It is a* **conjunction** and so the pronouns following it must be used carefully ; as—
1. He has been more successful *than* **me**. *(incorrect)*

He has been more successful *than* **I** (*have been*). *(correct)*

He likes my brother more than **me**. *(correct)*

It means that *he likes my brother* **more than** *he likes me.*

B. GERUND, PARTICIPLE

A Gerund and a Participle must never be confused ; as—
1. We must forbid *him* coming. *(incorrect)*

We must forbid **his** coming. *(correct)*

LIE, LAY

These two verbs must not be confused. They have different meanings and forms :

Lie = *to be in a flat position*. Its forms are : Lie   lay   lain

But **Lay** = *put* or *place*. Its forms are : lay   laid   laid

SUCH, SAME

These two pronouns must be followed by **as** ; as—

1. This is the **same** man **as** we met yesterday.
2. **Such** persons **as** who are honest are respected everywhere.

HELP

Help is followed by a **gerund** ; as—

1. I could not *help* **laughing**.

OWING TO, DUE TO

Owing to = *because of*. It can be followed by any noun ; as—

Owing to unfavourable **circumstances**, we shall have to leave early. (*correct*)

But **due to** is always followed by an **abstract noun** because due is an *adjective* ; as—

1. *Due to* **overwork** his health failed.
2. The garden looks untidy *due to* the gardener's **absence**.

WISHES

If or **only if** are followed by **were** or **had been** ;

1. *If* I *was* he, I should do it. (*incorrect*)

   If I **were** he, I should do it. (*correct*)
2. I wish it *was* over. (*incorrect*)

   I wish it **were** over. (*correct*)

TEST YOURSELF

A. Correct each sentence :

1. A diamond ring, presented by her friends, were on view.

   ....

2. The team was about to take their positions in the field.

   ....

3. Let he and she be careful not to make such mistakes.
   ....

4. Who were you talking to in the room ?
   ....

5. Such rules do not apply to you and I.
   ....

6. This is one of the most interesting stories that has been heard.
   ....

7. The monsoon failed which caused a terrible famine.
   ....

8. He advised each of us to look after our healths.
   ....

9. Nobody rose to offer their seat to her.
   ....

10. Neither of them were ready to face the problem.
    ....

11. People now do not save their money like they used to do earlier.
    ....

12. My friend is more handsome than me.
    ....

13. Erika was more beautiful than any queen.
    ....

14. If such a proposal were made, we should accept it.
    ....

15. The journey by bus is as quick, perhaps quicker, than by train.
    ....

16. We should be glad if you will attend to this matter
    ....

17. She is the tallest of the two girls.
    ....

18. In spite of all his faults, I cannot but like him.
   ....

19. In this old age even, I prefer working hard than amusing myself.
   ....

20. He has failed the test due to his careless habits.
   ....

21. I was unable to find a house suitable for my wife and I.
   ....

22. Hardly had he come than he was recalled.
   ....

23. The king, with his family members, were present there.
   ....

24. The ten first pages of the book were missing.
   ....

25. He will not go to the movie without your coming too.
   ....

26. The quality of films are very inferior these days.
   ....

27. Each of the two things have their advantages.
   ....

28. One learns to discipline himself in the army.
   ....

29. Theirs was the finest house I have ever seen.
   ....

30. He hadn't ought to do it.
   ....

31. I didn't use to go for a morning walk.
   ....

32. They accompanied my brother and I.
   ....

33. Neither his sister nor his brother were able to help him.
....

34. I cannot open the drawer in which I put my pen in.
....

35. Of the two candidates, one was trying the hardest.
....

36. He was no more guilty than I.
....

37. No sooner had he arrived when he was taken to the rest house.
....

38. The roads are lined with trees just like New York.
....

39. Neither of these two books are useful to me.
....

40. Whom did you think he was ?
....

41. Who did you see coming in ?
....

42. Each town has it's own system of water-supply.
....

43. These curtains need coming down.
....

44. It all depends on them coming in time.
....

45. My friend is more capable than me to solve such problems.
....

46. Each of us was carrying his kit oneself.
....

47. This problem looks equally serious than that.
....

21 FIGURES OF SPEECH

It is a hard fact that in speaking and in writing, we want to impress the listener/reader as far as we can. So, we try to use impressive words or phrases in our speech/writing. These phrases or words are called **figures of speech**. Let us study some of them.

1. ## SIMILE

    Remember the following points :
    1. *This figure of speech is based on* **comparison**.
    2. We know that we generally *compare things of the* **same kind**.
    3. But in a **simile**, we *compare things of* **different kinds**.
    4. These different things **have one common point.**

    Examples :

    A **ship** sails (travels) on a sea.

    A **camel** runs (travels) in a desert.

    Both are different but they have **one common feature.**

    One can **use a simile** to describe this common feature as under :

    A *camel* is *like* a *ship* of the desert.

    A *simile* **is a statement of** *likeness* **between two things of different kinds having one common feature.**

    ☞ We use the word *like* or *as* to use a simile.

2. ## METAPHOR

    Remember the following points :
    1. *This figure of speech is also based on* **comparison**.
    2. It also compares two things of **different kinds**.
    3. These different things have **one common point**.
    4. But a metaphor **goes a step further.** It does not describe a thing to be like another thing. But **it describes a thing to be the other.**

    So, we can **use a metaphor** to describe the common feature of a *camel* and a *ship* as under :

    The *camel* **is the ship** of the desert.

    A *metaphor* **is the** *implied form* **of one thing** *seen into* **another.**

    ☞ A metaphor uses no introductory word (*like*, *as*, etc.)

To know the difference between a *simile* and a *metaphor*, study the following examples carefully :

	Simile	*Metaphor*
1.	Her face is *like the moon*.	*His face is the moon*.
2.	Mark was as brave *as a lion*.	Mark was *the lion* of Australia.
3.	Tom was *as fierce as a tiger*.	Tom was *the tiger* of Cairo.
4.	Shakespeare was *like J.K.Rowling*.	Shakespeare was *the J.K.Rowling* of England.
5.	Taylor *is as strong as George*.	Taylor is *the George* of Italy.

PERSONIFICATION

This figure of speech describes **non-living things** as **living things**.

1. "Have you lost your sting, *O Death* ?" asked the widow.
2. "Why are you silent today, *O Cave* ?" asked the jackal.

PARADOX

In this figure of speech a **true fact** is stated *in opposite terms* ; as—

1. Stone walls do not make a prison.
2. The child is father to the man.

HYPERBOLE

In this figure of speech a fact is stated **in exaggerated terms** ; as—

1. I loved my sister : even the love of forty thousand brothers for their sisters could not equal my love.

TEST YOURSELF

Name the *figure of speech* used in each statement :

1. I wandered lonely as a cloud. ....
2. Virtue is a rich treasure indeed. ....
3. Mercy drops like gentle rain-drops. ....
4. Why don't you cleave to hear this, O Earth ? ....
5. Iron bars do not make a cage. ....
6. Jackson is the vulture of the state. ....
7. The red rose looks like a blushing damsel. ....
8. It is a pious fraud. ....
9. It is a white lie. ....
10. Our soldiers were swifter than eagles and stronger than lions. ....

22 VOCABULARY

A. DIMINUTIVES

Word	Diminutive	Word	Diminutive	Word	Diminutive
1. animal	animalcule	16. dear	darling	31. pile	pillow
2. ankle	anklet	17. face	facet	32. pouch	pocket
3. arm	armlet	18. globe	globule	33. river	rivulet
4. art	article	19. grain	granule	34. sack	satchel
5. babe	baby	20. hill	hillock	35. seed	seedling
6. ball	bullet	21. home	hamlet	36. shade	shadow
7. bird	birdie	22. isle	islet	37. sign	signet
8. book	booklet	23. leaf	leaflet	38. song	sonnet
9. bull	bullock	24. lock	locket	39. table	tablet
10. cabin	cabinet	25. maid	maiden	40. thick	thicket
11. cart	chariot	26. mole	molecule	41. tower	turret
12. cigar	cigarette	27. mouth	muzzle	42. vase	vessel
13. crown	coronet	28. nose	nozzle	43. cut	cutlet
14. dad	daddy	29. pack	packet	44. young	youngster
15. dame	damsel	30. part	particle		

B. ONE-WORD SUBSTITUTES

A. Murders

1. murder of *one's mother* — **matricide**
2. murder of *one's father* — **patricide**
3. murder of *one's brother* — **fratricide**
4. murder of *oneself* — **suicide**
5. murder of a *human-being* — **homicide**
6. murder of an *infant* — **infanticide**
7. murder of the *king* — **regicide**

8.	murder of pests	**pesticide**
9.	murder of ill germs	**germicide**

B. Food-Eaters

10.	a person who lives on plant food	**vegetarian**
11.	a person who takes animal food	**non-vegetarian**
12.	an animal that lives on flesh	**carnivore**
13.	an animal that lives on herbs	**herbivore**
14.	an animal that lives on grass	**grassivore**
15.	an animal that lives on fish	**piscivore**
16.	a person who eats human flesh	**cannibal**

C. Believers

17.	a person who believes in God	**theist**
18.	a person who does not believe in God	**atheist**
19.	a person who worships one God	**monotheist**
20.	a person who worships many gods	**polytheist**

D. Lovers and Haters

21.	one who loves the bright side of things	**optimist**
22.	one who loves the dark side of things	**pessimist**
23.	one who loves extreme steps	**extremist**
24.	one who loves alarming others	**alarmist**
25.	one who practises dentistry	**dentist**
26.	one who loves cycling	**cyclist**
27.	one who loves mankind	**philanthropist**
28.	one who hates mankind	**misanthropist**
29.	one who hates women	**misogynist**
30.	one who loves women	**philogynist**

E. Writings

31.	beautiful writing	**calligraphy**
32.	written life-story of a person	**biography**
33.	life-story of a person written by himself or herself	**autobiography**

F. Sciences

34.	science of plants	**botany**
35.	science of the behaviour of heavenly bodies	**astronomy**
36.	science of the development of mankind	**anthropology**
37.	science of the study of various races of mankind	**ethnology**
38.	science of the human body	**physiology**
39.	science of the human mind	**psychology**
40.	science of animals	**zoology**
41.	science of living-beings	**biology**
42.	science of elements	**chemistry**
43.	science of material things	**physics**
44.	earth's gaseous air-coat	**atmosphere**
45.	science of the earth's surface	**geography**
46.	science of the different layers of the earth	**geology**
47.	science of reading hands	**palmistry**

G. Adjectives

48.	worthy of living	**liveable**
49.	according to the law of the land	**legal**
50.	against the law of the land	**illegal**
51.	that can be seen	**visible**
52.	that cannot be seen	**invisible**
53.	that can be moved	**movable**
54.	that cannot be moved	**immovable**
55.	that can be heard	**audible**
56.	that cannot be heard	**inaudible**
57.	that can be described	**describable**
58.	that cannot be described	**indescribable**
59.	that can be corrected	**corrigible**
60.	that cannot be corrected	**incorrigible**
61.	that can be changed	**changeable**

62.	that cannot be changed	unchangeable
63.	that can be read	legible
64.	that cannot be read	illegible
65.	that dissolves in liquid	soluble
66.	that does not dissolve in liquid	insoluble
67.	worthy of loving	lovable
68.	about the age of marrying	marriageable
69.	worthy of wedding	weddable

H. Government

70.	government by a king	monarchy
71.	government by the few	oligarchy
72.	government by the people	democracy

I. Substances

73.	easily breakable	brittle
74.	that can easily bend	flexible
75.	through which light can pass	transparent
76.	through which light cannot pass	opaque

C. DOUBLE DERIVATIVES DISTINGUISHED

1. **affection, affectation**

   Both the words are derived from **affect**.

   Affection means love while affectation means pretence.
   - (a) A mother has deep *affection* for her children.
   - (b) Beware of his *affectations*. He is a rascal indeed.

2. **alternate, alternative**

   Both the words are derived from **alter**.

   Alternate means occurring by turns while alternative means another choice.
   - (a) I go to see him on *alternate* days.
   - (b) Charles had no *alternative* to leaving Britain.

3. **born, borne**

    Both the words are derived from **bear**.

    Born refers to birth while borne means carried

    (a) A son was *born* to him in his ripe old age.

    (b) The dead body was *borne* to the cemetery.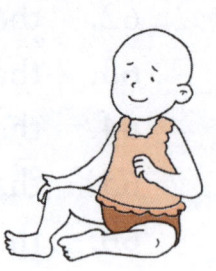

4. **continual, continuous**

    Both the words are derived from **continue**.

    Continual means frequent, i.e. occurring after intervals but continuous means constant.

    (a) *Continual* attacks of fever have ruined my health.

    (b) *Continuous* rain for two hours has flooded the streets.

5. **destiny, destination**

    Both the words are derived from **destine**.

    Destiny means fate while destination means goal.

    (a) *Destiny* has been very cruel to me.

    (b) We reached our *destination* safe and sound.

6. **estimate, estimation**

    Both the words are derived from **esteem**.

    estimate means rough calculation while estimation means judgement.

    (a) *Estimate* of expenditure on this building is very high.

    (b) In my *estimation*, he is a perfect gentleman.

7. **expanse, expansion**

    Both the words are derived from **expand**.

    Expanse means extent of expanding while expansion means act of expanding.

    (a) A sea is a vast *expanse* of water.

    (b) Heat causes *expansion* in metallic objects.

8. **industrial, industrious**

    Both the words are derived from **industry**.

    Industrial means pertaining to industry while industrious means hardworking.

    (a) Kent is the largest *industrial* centre in the United States.

(b) Villagers are generally more *industrious* than townsmen.

9. **insure, ensure**

   Both the words are derived from **sure**.

   Insure means to assure one's life while ensure means to make sure.

   (a) He is *insured* for a sum of five lakh dollars.

   (b) I have paid three months' fees to *ensure* my admission.

10. **lovely, lovable**

    Both the words are derived from **love**.

    Lovely means charming while lovable means worthy of love.

    (a) What a *lovely* flower it is !

    (b) Henry is a *lovable* child indeed.

11. **observance, observation**

    Both the words are derived from **observe**.

    Observance means acting upon while observation means a careful look.

    (a) *Observance* of these rules is necessary for discipline.

    (b) She has a very keen *observation*.

12. **popular, populous**

    Both the words are derived from **people**.

    Popular means liked by the people while populous means thickly populated.

    (a) He is the most *popular* teacher in our school.

    (b) New York is the most *populous* city of America.

13. **receipt, reception**

    Both the words are derived from **receive**.

    Receipt means receiving a thing while reception refers to receiving a person.

    (a) Issue me a *receipt* for this amount.

    (b) The leader was given a warm *reception*.

14. **respectful, respectable**

    Both the words are derived from **respect**.

    Respectful means showing respect while respectable means worthy of respect.

(a) He is a *respectful* child.

(b) She comes of a *respectable* family.

15. **union, unity**
Both the words are derived from **unit**.
Union means combination while unity means oneness.

(a) *Union* is strength.

(b) A prime number has no factor except itself and *unity*.

D. IMPORTANT PREFIXES

	Prefixes		Meanings	Examples
1.	a-	=	on, in, up	ashore, asleep, awake
2.	al-	=	all	almost, almighty, already
3.	auto-	=	self	automatic, autobiogarphy
4.	be-, em-	=	make or cause	befool, empower
5.	en-, im-	=	„ „ „	ensure, imprison
6.	bi-	=	two	bicycle, biped
7.	de-	=	down	dethrone, descend
8.	dis-	=	not	displease, disobey, disrespect
9.	ill-	=	not	illegal, illiterate
10.	im-	=	not	immortal, immovable, immodest
11.	in-	=	not	incorrect, incomplete, infirm
12.	ir-	=	not	irresponsible, irregular
13.	un-	=	not	uncommon, unkind, unable
14.	fore-	=	before	forehead, foretell
15.	mis-	=	bad	misuse, misdeed
16.	over-	=	excess	over-ripe, overdo, overact

E. IMPORTANT SUFFIXES

(a) TO FORM NOUNS

	Suffixes	Examples		Suffixes	Examples
1.	-ar, -er, -or	liar, speaker, actor	2.	-age	marriage, carriage

3.	-ancy, -ency	vacancy, emergency	4.	dom	wisdom, kingdom
5.	-hood	childhood, manhood	6.	-ment	movement, treatment
7.	-ness	happiness, kindness	8.	-ship	friendship, hardship
9.	-ice	cowardice	10.	-y	beggary, honesty
11.	-ty	cruelty, surety	12.	-red	hatred, learned
13.	-th	truth, width	14.	-tion	protection, action

(b) TO FORM VERBS

Suffixes	Examples	Suffixes	Examples
15. -ate	vacate, tabulate	18. -se	cleanse, rinse
16. -le	twinkle, wrinkle	19. -ish	perish, blackish
17. -en	widen, soften	20. -fy	beautify, amplify

(c) TO FORM ADJECTIVES

Suffixes	Examples	Suffixes	Examples
21. -y	thirsty, needy	30. -an	German, European
22. -al	central, final	31. -ese	Chinese, Japanese
23. -able	lovable, changeable	32. -ic	heroic, classic
24. -ible	sensible, terrible	33. -less	hopeless, useless
25. -ant	vacant, secant	34. -like	childlike, fairy-like
26. -ent	obedient, different	35. -ly	kingly, manly
27. -en	golden, woollen	36. -some	quarrelsome
28. -ern	northern, southern	37. -ous	glorious, famous
29. -ful	careful, useful		

F. COMMON ERRORS

A. AGREEMENT OF THE VERB WITH ITS SUBJECT

	Incorrect	Correct
(a) 1.	He *don't* like to be punished.	He **doesn't** like to be punished.
2.	This kind of mangoes *are* sweet.	This kind of mangoes **is** sweet.
3.	There *stands* Peter and Mark.	There **stand** Peter and Mark.
4.	Here *come* their mummy.	Here **comes** their mummy.

	Incorrect	Correct
(b) 5.	Bread and butter *are* perfect foods.	Bread and butter **is** a perfect food.
6.	The horse and carriage *are* at the door.	The horse and carriage **is** at the door.
7.	The great dancer and singer *are* dead.	The great dancer and singer **is** dead.
(c) 8.	Each of us *are* honest.	Each of us **is** honest.
9.	Either of the two friends *are* at fault.	Either of the two friends **is** at fault.
10.	Neither of the two girls *are* pretty.	Neither of the two girls **is** pretty.
11.	Everybody should do *their* duty.	Everybody should do **his/her** duty.
(d) 12.	Twenty kilometres *are* a long distance.	Twenty kilometres **is** a very long distance.
13.	Fifty hundred dollars *are* a small amount.	Fifty hundred dollars **is** a small amount.
14.	The United States *are* a big country.	The United States **is** a big country.
15.	Much *have been* done for you.	Much **has been** done for you.
16.	Little *have been* done so far.	Little **has been** done so far.

B. ERRORS IN THE USE OF NOUNS

	Incorrect	Correct
1.	He has *many works* to do.	He has **much work** to do.
2.	I gave him *many advices*.	I gave him **much advice.**
3.	These *furnitures* are very fine.	This **furniture** is very fine.
4.	The *sceneries* of Switzerland *are* very charming.	The **scenery** of Switzerland is very charming.
5.	She has read *many poetries*.	She has read **many poems**.
6.	The news of her death *are true*.	The news of her death **is true**.
7.	Her hair *are* curly.	Her hair **is** curly.
8.	I have five grey *hair* on my head.	I have five grey **hairs** on my head.
9.	The cattle *is* grazing.	The cattle **are** grazing.
10.	Mathematics *are* a tough subject.	Mathematics **is** a tough subject.
11.	Fruits *were served* after the dinner.	Fruit **was served** after the dinner.
12.	Green vegetable *is good* for health.	Green vegetables **are good** for health.

	Incorrect	*Correct*
13.	He gave me *an advice*.	He gave me **some advice** (or a **piece of advice**).
14.	The road is under *repair*.	The road is under **repairs**.
15.	He is a *man of word*.	He is a **man of his word**.
16.	I have my *meal* at 1 p.m.	I have my **meals** at 1 p.m.
17.	I have read *two-third* of the book.	I have read **two-thirds** of the book.
18.	He is one of the *best boy* in the class.	He is one of the **best boys** in the class.
19.	I *bought a blotting* and she bought *a copy*.	I **bought a blotting-paper** and she bought a **copy-book**.
20.	We are leaving by *10-30 o'clock train*.	We are leaving by **10-30 train**.
21.	There is no *place for you* on this bench.	There is no **room for you** on this bench.

C. ERRORS IN THE USE OF PRONOUNS

	Incorrect	*Correct*
1.	*Yours loving* son.	**Your loving** son.
2.	*Your obediently*.	**Yours obediently**.
3.	Never keep *yourself away* from school.	Never **keep away** from school.
4.	I feel *myself unwell* today.	I feel **unwell today**.
5.	I *enjoyed a* lot at Japan.	I **enjoyed myself** a lot at Japan.
6.	Tell me *who you met*.	Tell me **whom you met**.
7.	Tell me *whom met you*.	Tell me **who met you**.
8.	*Which is the taller*—Mac or Fred?	**Who is the taller**—Mac or Fred?
9.	*Each of the two* girls is pretty.	**Either of the two** girls is pretty.
10.	*None of the two* girls is slim.	**Neither of the two** girls is slim.
11.	Mac and Liz love *one another*.	Mac and Liz love **each other**.
12.	All men should love *each other*.	All men should love **one another**.
13.	*I, he* and *you* will go for a picnic.	**You, he** and **I** will go for a picnic.
14.	*You, he* and *I* are at fault.	**I, you** and **he** are at fault.

	Incorrect	correct
15.	You and *me* shall *go* there.	You and **I** shall **go** there.
16.	I like both you and *he*.	I like both you and **him**.
17.	Let *they try* once more.	Let **them try** once more.
18.	It is I, sir.	It is **me**, sir.
19.	Mac is taller than *me*.	Mac is taller than **I**.
20.	She is as good as *him*.	She is as good as **he**.
21.	They know it as well as *us*.	They know it as well as **we**.
22.	One must do *his* duty.	One must do **one's duty**.
23.	Your shirt is finer than *my*.	Your shirt is finer than **mine**.
24.	*Your this pen* is very fine.	**This pen of yours** is very fine.
25.	Where is *mine* book ?	Where is **my** book ?
26.	You and he have done *their* work.	You and he have done **your** work.
27.	You and I have done *your* work.	You and I have done **our** work.

D. ERRORS IN THE USE OF ADJECTIVES

1.	This tree is *very large* than that.	This tree is **larger** than that.
2.	Woodsworth is greater than *all poets*.	Woodsworth is greater than any **other poet**.
3.	Mac is the *wisest* of the two.	Mac is the **wiser** of the two.
4.	Who is *taller*—you or he ?	Who is **the taller**—you or he?
5.	Todd is *more* wiser than his brother.	Todd is **much** wiser than his brother.
6.	My horse is *the most* swiftest horse.	My horse is **by far the** swiftest.
7.	This pen is superior *than* that.	This pen is superior **to** that.
8.	He is junior *than* me by two years.	He is junior **to** me by two years.
9.	I prefer this pen *than* that.	I prefer this pen **to** that.
10.	No *less than* five boys are in the room.	No **fewer than** five boys are in the room.
11.	She feeds *the poors* daily.	She feeds **the poor** daily.
12.	I shall give you *many informations*.	I shall give you **much information**.
13.	The jug has *any* milk.	The jug has **some** milk.

	Incorrect	Correct
14.	The jug has *no any* milk.	The jug **has no** milk.
15.	I have a *strong* headache.	I have a **severe** headache.
16.	I thank you for your *such* help.	I thank you for your **timely** help.
17.	Never go out *open-headed*.	Never go out **bare-head**.
18.	I met him *on that* day.	I met him **the other** day.
19.	I have *many pounds*.	I have **much money**.
20.	He is my *older* brother.	He is my **elder** brother.
21.	Speak *a bit more* loudly.	Speak **a bit louder**.
22.	She is *enough rich* to afford for it.	She is **rich enough** to afford for it.
23.	*A little* boys are as good as Mark.	**A few** boys are as good as Mark.
24.	He is very *high*.	He is very **tall**.

E. ERRORS IN THE USE OF A, AN, THE

	Incorrect	Correct
1.	He is *a* M.A.	He is **an** M.A.
2.	He is *a* honest man.	He is **an** honest man.
3.	I bought *an* uniform.	I bought **a** uniform.
4.	*An one-eyed man* lived there.	**A one-eyed man** lived there.
5.	She had sound sleep.	She had **a** sound sleep.
6.	The *cows are* milch *animals*.	The **cow is** a milch **animal**.
7.	*Horse* is a faithful animal.	**The horse** is a faithful animal.
8.	*Himalayas is* the highest mountain.	**The Himalayas are** the highest mountains.
9.	*Earth* is very hot inside.	**The earth** is very hot inside.
10.	*The Rome* is in Italy.	**Rome** is in Italy.
11.	*The gold* is a costly metal.	**Gold** is a costly metal.
12.	*The beauty* needs no ornaments.	**Beauty** needs no ornaments.
13.	*Father and son* rode the donkey.	**The father and the son** rode the donkey.
14.	A white and black cow *were* grazing.	A white and black cow **was** grazing.
15.	*The English* is the language *of English*.	**English** is the language **of the English**.

	Incorrect	Correct
16.	I have never *seen a such* good picture.	I have never **seen such a** good picture.
17.	He spent *all money* he had.	He spent **all the money** he had.
18.	There are *good many* tigers in this forest.	There are **a good many** tigers in this forest.
19.	*A man* is mortal.	**Man** is mortal.
20.	What kind *of a boy* is he ?	What kind **of boy** is he ?
21.	This *is a news* to me.	This **is news** to me.
22.	*What fool* you are !	**What a fool** you are !
23.	I *feel pain* in my back.	I **feel a pain** in my back.
24.	I caught him *by his neck*.	I caught him **by the neck**.
25.	This is *a pen* I want.	This is **the pen** I want.

F. ERRORS IN THE USE OF VERBS

	Incorrect	Correct
1.	She *has arrived* yesterday.	She **arrived** yesterday.
2.	I *am studying* here since 1990.	I **have been studying** here since 1990.
3.	We *did not see* you for a long time.	We **have not seen** you for a long time.
4.	This book *is belong* to her.	This book **belongs** to her.
5.	I *am fail in* the test.	I **have failed** the test.
6.	He *is pass in* the test.	He **has passed** the test.
7.	Her father *is died*.	Her father **has died**.
8.	Before I reached the office, everybody *came*.	Before I reached the office, everybody **had come**.
9.	Why *you are going* to Canada ?	Why **are you going** to Canada ?
10.	Let me know why *are you* late.	Let me know why **you are** late.
11.	The queen enquired if the king *is* alive.	The queen enquired if the king **was** alive.
12.	She said that *I will come*.	She said that **she would come**.

	Incorrect	Correct
13.	*Can I come* in, sir?	**May I come** in, sir?
14.	Yes, I *may* solve this sum.	Yes, I **can** solve this sum.
15.	*Keep* this book on the table.	**Place** this book on the table.
16.	Erika *sung* a sweet song.	Erika **sang** a sweet song.
17.	Stop *to talk*.	Stop **talking**.
18.	*I have and* will again *say* so.	I have **said** and will again say so.
19.	I know *him a good* boy.	I know **him to be a good** boy.
20.	This water is not fit *for drinking*.	This water is not fit **to drink**.
21.	I forbade him *from going there*.	I forbade him **to go there**.
22.	He succeeded *to win* a prize.	He succeeded **in winning** a prize.
23.	I want a chair *for sitting* on.	I want a chair **to sit** on.
24.	He resembles *to his* father.	He resembles **his** father.
25.	We *went to home*.	We **went home**.
26.	I cannot *help for* it.	I cannot **help it**.
27.	He always *tells* the truth.	He always **speaks** the truth.
28.	He is *speaking* a lie.	He is **telling** a lie.
29.	He *said* me a fool.	He **called** me a fool.
30.	*Open* this knot.	**Untie** this knot.
31.	*Cut* this pencil, please.	**Mend** this pencil, please.
32.	Columbus *invented* America.	Columbus **discovered** America.
33.	Let him *lay* there.	Let him **lie** there.
34.	The traveller *laid down* under a tree.	The traveller **lay down** under a tree.
35.	I *hope* he will not pass the test.	I **fear** he will not pass the test.
36.	I *ate* my dinner.	I **had** my dinner.
37.	I *sleep* at 10:00 p.m.	I **go to bed** at 10:00 p.m.
38.	She *begot* a daughter.	She **bore** a daughter.
39.	The murderer *was hung*.	The murderer **was hanged**.
40.	The teacher *took* us a test in English.	The teacher **gave** us a test in English.

	Incorrect	Correct
41.	We *gave* a test in English.	We **took** a test in English.
42.	*Bring* me a cup of tea.	**Fetch** me a cup of tea.
43.	The ship *was drowned*.	The ship **sank**.
44.	The *crew sank*.	The **crew were drowned**.
45.	*Hear her* advice.	**Listen to her** advice.
46.	I *said* him good night.	I **wished** him good night.
47.	We *said to her* good-bye.	We **bade her** good-bye.
48.	I shall *stop* with my brother at his place.	I shall **stay** with my brother at his place.
49.	He *denied* to pardon me.	He **refused** to pardon me.
50.	The goalkeeper *protected* the goal.	The goalkeeper **defended** the goal.
51.	*Find this word* in the dictionary.	**Look up this word** in the dictionary.
52.	A heavy log was *swimming* in water.	A heavy log was **floating** in water.
53.	Fish *float* in the sea.	Fish **swim** in the sea.
54.	*Thanks* God.	**Thank** God.

G. ERRORS IN THE USE OF ADVERBS

	Incorrect	Correct
1.	It is *too* cold today.	It is **very** cold today.
2.	He is *very* weak to move about.	He is **too** weak to move about.
3.	This story is *much* interesting.	This story is **very** interesting.
4.	He is *very* obliged to me.	He is **much** obliged to me.
5.	It was *very* hotter yesterday than today.	It was **much** hotter yesterday than today.
6.	People left the hall *by and by*.	People left the hall **one by one**.
7.	The bus has *arrived immediately*.	The bus has **arrived just now**.
8.	She will reach here *just now*.	She will reach here **presently**.
9.	Do you *know to swim*?	Do you **know how to swim**?
10.	The load is *too much* heavy.	The load is **much too** heavy.
11.	Sleep is *quite necessary* for health.	Sleep is **very necessary** for health.

	Incorrect	Correct
12.	He is *very satisfied* with your work.	He is **quite satisfied** with your work.
13.	We feel *much tired*.	We feel **very tired**.
14.	She is *somewhat tall* for her age.	She is **rather tall** for her age.

H. ERRORS IN THE USE OF PREPOSITIONS

	Incorrect	Correct
1.	Distribute these mangoes *between* all the boys.	Distribute these mangoes **among** all the boys.
2.	Divide this money *among* the two brothers.	Divide this money **between** the two brothers.
3.	I have been very busy *for* Monday.	I have been very busy **since** Monday.
4.	We shall start this work *from* Monday next.	We shall start this work **on** Monday next.
5.	I shall be free *since* evening today.	I shall be free **by** evening today.
6.	He lives *at* New Zealand.	He lives **in** New Zealand.
7.	He is in home.	He is **at** home.
8.	A fox fell *in* a well.	A fox fell **into** a well.
9.	The milk is *into* the jug.	The milk is **in** the jug.
10.	The shepherd cried *on* the top of his voice.	The shepherd cried **at** the top of his voice.
11.	He is sitting *upon* a stool.	He is sitting **on** a stool.
12.	The leopard sprang *on* the deer.	The leopard sprang **at** the deer.
13.	I shall return *after* a week.	I shall return **in** a week.
14.	We shall finish this job *before* three days.	We shall finish this job **within** three days.
15.	I have bought this pen *at* $ 1.	I have bought this pen **for** $ 1.
16.	I bought apples 5 for a pound.	I bought apples **at** 5 for a pound.
17.	The sugar sells *by* $1 a kg.	The sugar sells **at** $1 a kg.
18.	We warned him *about* the danger.	We warned him **of** the danger.

	Incorrect	Correct
19.	She went *back to home*.	She went **back home**.
20.	What is the time *in* your watch?	What is the time **by** your watch?
21.	He is angry *on* me.	He is angry **with** me.
22.	She is angry *with* your behaviour.	She is angry **at** your behaviour.
23.	Sally was married *with* James.	Sally was married **to** James.
24.	She has come *in a* train.	She has come **by** train.
25.	The guest is sitting *on* an arm-chair.	The guest is sitting **in** an arm-chair.
26.	Compare Sam *to* Tony.	Compare Sam **with** Tony.
27.	They accused him *with* murder.	They accused him **of** murder.
28.	He *reached* at the station.	He **arrived** at the station.
29.	You must reach there *before* 10 o'clock.	You must reach there **by** 10 o'clock.
30.	We *entered into the* room one by one.	We **entered the** room one by one.
31.	You must return *till* tomorrow.	You must return **by** tomorrow.
32.	He was appointed *as a* clerk.	He was appointed **a** clerk.
33.	I say it *at* your face.	I say it **to** your face.
34.	Copy this para word *by* word.	Copy this para word **for** word.
35.	This book is different *than* that.	This book is different **from** that.
36.	This pen is superior *than* that.	This pen is superior **to** that.
37.	His brother died *from* fever.	His brother died **of** fever.
38.	Tie the horse *with a* tree.	Tie the horse **to a** tree.
39.	He repented *for* his folly.	He repented **of** his folly.
40.	He *pocketed up* the insult.	He **pocketed the** insult.

I. ERRORS IN THE USE OF CONJUNCTIONS

	Incorrect	Correct
1.	When I reached home, *then* I took rest.	When I reached home, I took rest.
2.	If you work hard, *then you* will pass.	If you work hard, you will pass.
3.	As I am ill, *so* I cannot come.	As I am ill, I cannot come.
4.	Though he is poor *but* he is honest.	Though he is poor, **yet** he is honest.

5. It *is* a week since it rained. — It **has been** a week since it rained.
6. He will not pass, unless *he doesn't work hard*. — He will not pass unless **he works hard**.
7. She asked me *that why* I was weeping. — She asked me **why** I was weeping.

G. NOTE THE DIFFERENCE

1. Tenzing conquered Mt. Everest **alone**. (only this peak)
   Tenzing **alone** conquered Mt. Everest. (single-handed)
2. She is the **best teacher**. (best of all the teachers)
   She is the **best lady-teacher**. (best of all the female teachers)
3. The bus and the car reached **at the same time**. (together)
   The bus and the car reached **in the same time**. (took the same time to cover the distance)
4. I found the road **easy**. (the road was not tough)
   I found the road **easily**. (without any difficulty)
5. James is **my friend**. (refers to James only)
   James is a **friend of mine**. (one of many friends)
6. I gave the **beggar a half-dollar**. (50 cents)
   I gave the **beggar half a dollar**. (50 cents in any form)
7. I forgot **to do it**. (did not do it)
   I forgot **how to do it**. (the manner of doing it)
8. The student read the **first two chapters**. (the first and the second chapters of the same book)
   The student read the **two first chapters**. (the first chapter of either of the two books)
9. He has joined school **late**. (after the fixed date)
   He has joined school **lately**. (recently)
10. **Happily,** I have done the job. (luckily)
    I have done the job **happily**. (was happy to do it)
11. **At length,** I had a talk with her. (at last)
    I had a talk with her **at length**. (in detail)

12.	Mac **left** Australia on Sunday.	(went out of Australia)
	Mac **left for** Australia on Sunday.	(went to Australia)
13.	Alfred **deals the cards**.	(distributes them in a game)
	Alfred **deals in cards**.	(sells cards)
14.	The teacher **looked over** the matter.	(considered it)
	The teacher **overlooked** the matter.	(did not consider it)
15.	I **met** him on my way home.	(intentionally)
	I **met** him **up** on my way home.	(by chance)
16.	I **called** Richard.	(shouted to him)
	I **called on** Richard.	(saw him)
17.	He loves his **only son**.	(has no other son)
	He loves his **son only**.	(loves no other child)
18.	The hunter **shot a pigeon**.	(killed it)
	The hunter **shot at a pigeon**.	(fired at it)
19.	The hunter **shot a deer dead**.	(killed it)
	The hunter **shot a dead deer**.	(fired at an already dead deer)
20.	There is **room** for you here.	(space to sit)
	There is **a room** for you here.	(a room in a building)
21.	He returned **in no time**.	(very soon)
	He returned **at no time**.	(never)
22.	He is going to England **in a month**.	(after 30 days)
	He is going to England **within a month**.	(before 30 days are over)
23.	He is **well** now.	(in good health)
	He is **well-off** now.	(rich)
24.	Alfred visited me **every third day**.	(after every two days)
	Alfred visited me **every three days**.	(after every three days)
25.	Mac is his father's **eldest child**.	(born first of all)
	Mac is the **oldest child** in the family.	(oldest in age)
26.	**Search** the child.	(look into its pockets etc.)
	Search for the child.	(look for the child itself)
27.	My servant **works the machine**.	(drives the machine)
	My servant **works at the machine**.	(is a workman)

H. COMMON PHRASES AND IDIOMS

1. **break loose** = *get unchained*
   The cow *broke loose* and trampled the crop.

2. **break open** = *open by breaking*
   The thieves *broke open* the safe and looted the ornaments.

3. **come true** = *prove true*
   His dream of standing first has *come true*.

4. **come wrong** = *be inacceptable*
   A good dinner never *comes wrong* to anyone.

5. **cut short** = *come to an end*
   His life was *cut short* by a severe attack of cholera.

6. **fall flat** = *have no effect*
   My advice *fell flat* on him.

7. **fall short** = *be lower than expected*
   The result *fell short* of our expectations.

8. **fight shy** = *avoid coming in front*
   People often *fight shy* of involving in others' quarrels.

9. **get rid of** = *be free*
   I have not *got rid of* my problems so far.

10. **great hand** = *expert at*
    He is a great hand at organising public meetings.

11. **go mad/blind etc.** = *suffer*
    1. His pet dog has *gone mad*.
    2. My mother went *blind* three years before her death.

12. **go wrong** = *turn out harmful*
    Everything *went wrong* after the chairman's death.

13. **hold good** = *prove applicable*
    This rule does not *hold good* here.

14. **lay bare** = *discover; expose*
    The C.I.D. officer *laid bare* all the irregularities done by the cashier.

15. **lay waste** = *destroy*
    The invader *laid waste* almost the entire country.

16. **live fast** = *lead a rapid life*
   One who *lives fast* is sure to die early.
17. **look blank** = *be puzzled*
   When he came to know of his dismissal, he *looked blank*.
18. **look sharp** = *make haste; lose no time*
   Look sharp otherwise we shall be late.
19. **make good** = *compensate*
   You have caused me a big loss. So, you must make it good.
20. **make merry** = *have fun*
   Sailors like to *make merry* when they reach the shore.
21. **make sure** = *become sure*
   A wise man *makes sure* that his investment will not be lost in any case.
22. **make light (little) of** = *give no importance*
   He *made light of* the advice that I gave him.
23. **play false** = *cheat*
   A good salesman never *plays* his customers *false*.
24. **put (set) right** = *to place in order*
   Books are lying at sixes and sevens. *Set* them *right*.
25. **run short** = *become too little*
   The funds *ran short* and the business suffered a lot.
26. **stop short** = *stop where one is* "*Stop short*! Otherwise I shall shoot you," said the policeman to the running thief.
27. **take ill** = *fall ill*
   My father *took ill* and so I could not come to school.
28. **talk big** = *boast*
   Never *talk big* of yourself. It is sure to annoy God.

B. WORDS IN PAIRS :

29. **bag and baggage** = *with all the belongings*
   The rich man left the town *bag and baggage*.
30. **by fits and starts** = *in irregular spells*
   One who does things *by fits and starts* cannot achieve anything.
31. **by leaps and bounds** = *very fast*
   My business has progressed *by leaps and bounds*.

32. **fair and square** = *just*
    His uncle is quite *fair and square* in dealings.
33. **first and foremost** = *very first*
    Our *first and foremost* duty is towards our country.
34. **heart and soul** = *with full might and attention*
    He throws himself *heart and soul* into everything he does.
35. **over and above** = *in addition to*
    Over and above being diligent, he is honest.
36. **over head and ears** = *completely*
    I am *over head and ears* in debt.
37. **safe and sound** = *quite safe and unhurt*
    We arrived home quite *safe and sound*.
38. **stuff and nonsense** = *rubbish*
    What you have said is all *stuff and nonsense*.
39. **sum and substance** = *gist*
    This is the *sum and substance* of his speech.
40. **up and doing** = *ready to act*
    Be *up and doing* if you want to succeed.
41. **ways and means** = *necessary regulations and funds*
    Before starting a business be sure of its *ways and means*.
42. **well and good** = *O.K.*
    If that is your aim, it is *well and good*.
43. **will and pleasure** = *wish and satisfaction*
    I will act entirely according to your *will and pleasure*.
44. **might and main** = *as best as possible*
    We worked with *might and main* and were successful.

C. MORE PHRASES

45. **beck and call** = *motion (nod) of head*
    I am always at your *beck and call*.
46. **by hook or by crook** = *fair means or foul*
    I must gain my object *by hook or by crook*.
47. **hue and cry** = *noise*
    Seeing the fire, they raised a *hue and cry*.

48. **in fine** = *finally*
    In fine, we reached our destination.
49. **kith and kin** = *blood-relations*
    We are far away from all *kith and kin.*
50. **learn by rote** = *cram*
    It is no use *learning* anything *by rote.*
51. **lie in wait** = *sit in ambush*
    The tiger *lay in wait* for some prey.
52. **nick of time** = *critical moment*
    You have come to seek help in the *nick of time.*
53. **of no avail** = *with no effect*
    All my efforts were *of no avail* at all.
54. **on pain of** = *threatening with*
    He made me do it *on pain of* death.
55. **part and parcel** = *essential part*
    Being honest is a *part and parcel* of a plain life.
56. **spick and span** = *quite in order*
    Everything looked *spick and span* in the room.
57. **tit for tat** = *blow for blow*
    Some people believe in a *tit for tat* policy.
58. **as ever** = *ever before*
    He is as careless *as ever.*
59. **as usual** = *usually*
    As usual, I got up and went for a walk.
60. **thanks to** = *let us be thankful to*
    Thanks to the doctor, she has cured me.

I. SPECIAL PHRASES

1.	**bevy of girls/ladies**	never	*bevy of boys/gentlemen*
2.	**a bosom friend**	never	*a breast friend*
3.	**broad daylight**	never	*broad moonlight*
4.	**bright moonlight**	never	*bright daylight*
5.	**a fast friend**	never	*a fast enemy*
6.	**a golden age**	never	*a golden time/period*

7.	a leading question	never	a leading answer
8.	implicit faith	never	implicit love/hate
9.	a maiden speech	never	a maiden song
10.	a short cut	never	a short path
11.	standing army	never	a standing navy
12.	a sworn friend	never	a sworn enemy
13.	an avowed enemy	never	an avowed friend
14.	a tall talk	never	a lofty talk
15.	a lofty idea	never	a tall idea

J. COMPOUND ADJECTIVE PHRASES

1. **happy-go-lucky** = *carefree; cheerful*
   A *happy-go-lucky* person doesn't let anything worry him/her for long.

2. **out-of-date** = *not in pace with the time going on*
   These *out-of-date* ideas do not appeal to youngsters.

3. **out-and-out** = *thorough; complete*
   He looks an *out-and-out* crook.

4. **out-of-the-way** = *distant*
   It is not easy to reach this *out-of-the-way* place.

5. **out-of-doors** = *in the open*
   This *out-of-doors* plan can be carried out easily.

6. **hole-and-corner** = *secret*
   Some people favour a *hole-and-corner* policy by nature.

7. **stay-at-home** = *domestic (person)*
   He is a *stay-at-home* fellow and always shuns outings.

8. **go-ahead** = *pushing*
   Go-ahead persons always achieve their goals in life.

9. **stick-in-the-mud** = *static*
   A *stick-in-the-mud* person seldom achieves anything in life.

10. **upside-down** = *inverted*
    An *upside-down* thinking always proves harmful.

11. **null and void** = *having no force*
    An unsigned agreement is *null and void*.

TEST YOURSELF

A. Write a *single word* for the words printed in italics :

1. This writing is *such as cannot be read*.
   ....
2. Your plan *cannot be put into practice*.
   ....
3. He is not *fit for being elected* for this post.
   ....
4. The food is not *fit to be eaten*.
   ....
5. You *will have to respond* for your actions.
   ....
6. This scheme is *open to objections*.
   ....
7. These errors *cannot be corrected* at all.
   ....
8. Use of wine and tobacco *can cause injury* to health.
   ....
9. His manners are *more like those of a lady*.
   ....
10. He has *an evil reputation for cheating*.
    ....
11. He is a *man who hates women*.
    ....
12. This elderly person is a *lover of mankind*.
    ....

B. Write the *diminutive noun* for each of the following :

1. cart .... 2. table..............................
3. pouch.................................. 4. dame ....
5. maid .... 6. part ....
7. river .... 8. home ....

9. sign .... 10. hill ....
11. song .... 12. cigar ....

C. Explain the difference in meaning :

1. industrial, industrious
   (a) ....
   (b) ....

2. continual, continuous
   (a) ....
   (b) ....

3. notorious, famous
   (a) ....
   (b) ....

4. affection, affectation
   (a) ....
   (b) ....

5. accident, incident
   (a) ....
   (b) ....

6. swim, float
   (a) ....
   (b) ....

7. born, borne
   (a) ....
   (b) ....

8. respectful, respectable
   (a) ....
   (b) ....

D. Write the meaning of the *word in italics* in each sentence :

1. (a) I have never *remarked* this. = ...
   (b) The answer-sheet must be *re-marked*. = ...

2. (a) *Recount* your story, please. = ...
   (b) *Re-count* all these cents. = ...

3. (a) The seat is *reserved* for me. = ...
   (b) The guests were *re-served* with sweets. = ...

4. (a) *Replace* this book by that. = ...
   (b) *Re-place* this book on the shelf. = ...

E. Given below are two nouns formed from the same word. Write their meanings to show their difference :

1. Dear (a) dearness : ....
          (b) dearth : ....

2. Dry (a) dryness : ....
         (b) drought : ....

3. Slow (a) slowness : ....
          (b) sloth : ....

4. Graze (a) grass : ....
           (b) grazier : ....

5. True (a) truth : ....
          (b) trueness : ....

6. Read (a) reader : ....
          (b) reading : ....

7. Speak (a) speaker : ....
           (b) speech : ....

F. Use these idioms in your own sentences after writing the meaning of each :

1. well-off = ...
   ....
2. bag and baggage = ...
   ....
3. learn by rote = ...
   ....
4. play false = ...
   ....
5. stop short = ...
   ....
6. kith and kin = ...
   ....
7. on pain of = ...
   ....
8. hold true = ...
   ....
9. look sharp = ...
   ....
10. break loose = ...
    ....
11. fall flat = ...
    ....
12. by leaps and bounds = ...
    ....
13. first and foremost = ...
    ....
14. safe and sound = ...
    ....

23 WRITTEN COMPOSITION

A. PARAGRAPH WRITING

Let us write a paragraph on—**An Oasis**

An oasis is a green place in a dry desert. It has sand and sand all around. Sand-hills rise to height and enclose it on all sides. There is a pool of brackish water which tastes slightly salty. Palm trees grow around the pool to provide cool shade. Some green grass also grows over the land surrounding the pool. People of the desert build a few huts near the oasis. They keep camels, goats and sheep. They grow a few crops that provide food for them and fodder for their animals. An oasis is a resting place for travellers in the desert. They water their camels and also fill water in their bottles for use during the tough desert journey.

TEST YOURSELF

A. **Write a paragraph on—*The Scene at a Railway-Station.***

....

....

B. Write a paragraph on—*A Scene of a Desert*

24 PARAPHRASING

Paraphrasing means explaining a *piece of verse* in *prose*. Here is an example.

"I bring fresh showers,
For the thirsty flowers ;
From the seas and streams ;
I bear light shade,
For the leaves when laid,
In their mid-day dreams."

These lines describe the words of a cloud. It says that it causes fresh showers of rain for the thirsty plants and their flowers. It further explains that it brings water for the showers from seas and rivers. We know that water evaporates from these water-bodies to form clouds. In addition to this, the cloud says that it provides shade for the leaves of plants at noon when they require it the most to keep away from the hot sun.

TEST YOURSELF

A. Paraphrase the following verse in your own words :

Not a drum was heard, Not a funeral note,
And his corpse to the rampart we hurried ;
Not a soldier discharged his farewell shot,
Over the grave where our hero we buried.

....
....
....
....
....
....
....
....

B. Paraphrase the following verse :

Then whirling up his broad sword,
With both hands to the height ;
He rushed against Horatius,
And smote with all his might.

....
....
....
....
....
....
....
....

C. Paraphrase the following verse :

"Go, Lovely Rose !
Tell her that wastes her time and me,
That now she knows ;
When I resemble her to thee,
How sweet and fair she seems to be."

....
....
....
....
....
....
....
....

25 COMPREHENSION

The word—**comprehension**—means *the act of understanding*.

Comprehension trains the pupils for purposeful reading that enables them to digest whatever is read. It proves useful in day-to-day life in several ways :

1. It helps them to understand various problems.
2. It helps them to analyse those problems and their causes.
3. It helps them to write accurately whenever they have to.
4. It helps them to be practical in life.

Whenever you have to deal with a paragraph on comprehension, observe the following points carefully :

(a) Read the passage thoroughly and get the general idea contained in it.

(b) Read the passage again and underline the salient facts stated in it. It will help you answer the questions.

(c) Take up each question and put its number under the fact that suits best to be its answer.

(d) Now write the answers one by one such that each answer stands quite distinctly and does not overlap any other answer.

(f) Never add anything from yourself and express no personal views unless you have been asked to do so.

(g) Even if some words seem difficult to understand, stay cool. Read the passage over again and you will be able to guess the meaning of difficult words even.

(h) Write the answers briefly in correct short sentences of your own.

(i) Your answers must be to the point.

Let us have an example :

Read the paragraph given below and answer the questions given at its end :

Hardly had I settled down when the train started. I was in a mood to sing. But an elderly passenger was lying on a berth just opposite mine. I had just started crooning a tune when he fell fast asleep and began to snore heavily. So, I thought it wise not to disturb him. I kept watching the countryside that unrolled itself as the train sped along. Dry fields, ploughed fields, green fields, grazing cattle, mango groves, scattered villages, tall trees and thorny bushes were indeed a very charming sight to look at. After about two hours, the elderly man woke up. He cast a smiling look at me. I felt encouraged and sang a melodious song. Everybody around cheered me.

QUESTIONS :

1. What was the writer in a mood to do ?
2. Why did the writer stop crooning ?
3. What did the writer do then ?
4. What did the elderly man do when he woke up ?
5. What did the writer do then ?
6. What did the people sitting around do ?

ANSWERS :

1. The writer was in a mood to sing.
2. He stopped crooning because he didn't want to disturb the elderly man's sleep.
3. The writer kept watching the countryside out of the window of the running train.
4. The elderly man cast a smiling look at the writer.
5. The writer sang a melodious song.
6. People felt pleased to hear the song and they cheered the writer.

TEST YOURSELF

Read each of the following passages and answer the questions given at the end of each :

1.   Play is natural to children. There is no child that does not like to play. Even while teaching, if some playway method is followed, children learn things easily and with active interest. It is true especially for children who are just beginners. Not only this, play and games keep us active. And unless we are healthy, we cannot do any job in right earnest. Clearly, play, *i.e.* games and sports are so important for us. Isn't it a fact that people with certificates in

games and sports are given preference in almost every department ? The reason behind it that these people can prove helpful in case of any danger.

QUESTIONS:

1. Is there a child who does not like to play ?
   ....
2. How can play be useful in teaching-learning process ?
   ....
3. How is play useful to a person in general ?
   ....
4. How are sportsmen treated in every department ?
   ....
5. Why are sportsmen preferred in every department ?
   ....

2. A philosopher in Greece was asked why he wept over the death of his son when he preached that joy and sorrow were in vain. The philosopher replied, "I weep for wrong preaching only." And his answer became a hard fact. It can be only preached that we should never shed tears whatever the loss. But when it comes to reality, nobody can practise it. Sorrow unlocks the tears and they stream down the eyes. They have a balmy effect on the person who sheds them. They lessen the degree of the sorrow and wash the face. Without them, the dry sorrow is sure to parch the face and leads to furrows on it—the furrows that we call **wrinkles**.

QUESTIONS :

1. Who wept over the death of his son ?
   ....
2. What question was put to the philosopher ?
   ....
3. What answer did the philosopher give ?
   ....
4. What does sorrow do ?
   ....

5. How do tears affect the person who sheds them?
   ....

6. How can dry sorrow harm the face?
   ....

3. A short story is much more than a mere narrative of the happenings that took place. It has an underlying idea that is explained by the happenings or events. The dialogues in a story generally bring out its central idea clearly. They also clarify the personal views of the story-teller. If one reads through the story two or three times, its real theme will become quite clear. This theme may not be clear when one reads the story.

QUESTIONS:

1. Is a short story a mere narrative of events?
   ....

2. What is there underlying a story?
   ....

3. What brings out the central idea or theme of a story?
   ....

4. What more do the dialogues clarify?
   ....

5. When does the theme of a story become clear to the reader?
   ....

4. If a nation aims at being great as well as strong, it must have strong, brave wise, honest and diligent citizens. The strength of a nation lies in its men only. The quality of the citizens of a nation is the yard-stick that can measure its greatness. Some people think that a nation can be strong only if it has wealth. And wealth, they say, lies buried under the land. But who will tap that wealth? It is only the citizens of the nation that can tap this wealth. That is why it has been said—

Not gold but only men can make, A nation great and strong;

Men who for the nation's sake, Stand first and suffer long.

QUESTION :

1. How can a nation become strong ?
   ....
2. In what does the strength of a nation lie ?
   ....
3. What is the yard-stick for the greatness of a nation ?
   ....
4. Can money alone make a nation strong ?
   ....
5. Who can tap the underground wealth of a nation ?
   ....

5. As I was returning from school, I saw a large crowd of people gathered in front of a shop. Some people were shouting at each other. I went up to the place and saw that a quarrel was going on. It was between a shopkeeper and a customer. The customer had paid less money than demanded by the shopkeeper and so a dispute had arisen. First of all, they exchanged hot words but soon they began to trade blows. Seeing this, people assembled there and tried to pacify both the parties. It was with much difficulty that the matter came to be settled.

QUESTIONS :

1. Where was the writer returning from ?
   ....
2. Where had people gathered and why ?
   ....
3. Who were the parties in the quarrel ?
   ....
4. What was the cause of the quarrel ?
   ....
5. How was the quarrel settled ?
   ....

26 SUMMARIZING

A summary is the abridgement of a given paragraph in as few words as possible. The purpose of a summary is to present the gist of the given passage in a clear and brief form so that it may be easily understood and followed. Summary writing is a useful exercise. It increases the student's ability to grasp ideas quickly and accurately. At the same time, it gives practice in expressing ideas clearly and in a stylish way.

ESSENTIAL FEATURES OF A GOOD SUMMARY

A summary includes all the essential facts of the passage to be summarized. All the unimportant details are to be left out. Usually a summary is one third of the given passage in length. A good summary has five distinct features.

1. Accuracy 2. Clarity 3. Completeness 4. Compactness 5. Brevity

HOW TO WRITE A SUMMARY

1. Read the passage carefully—*several times if necessary*—to get its central idea.
2. Frame a suitable short title that should express the subject of the passage.
3. Go through the passage again and underline all the facts that are important for making the summary.
4. Number the facts and arrange them in proper order. It will give you an outline of the summary.
5. Go through the outline and strike out the points that can be still deleted.
6. Now write the summary. Make minimum use of the words and phrases of the given passage. Write it in your own words.
7. Always write the summary in the indirect speech. Be precise and to the point.
8. One word substitution is the best tool in summarizing passages.

Let us have an example.

EXAMPLE

The life of a cab driver is very hard indeed. He has to get up early and get his cab ready. He has to work the whole day long—be it scorching summer, icy-cold winter or muddy rainy season. He is a symbol of utter poverty. He knows no rest or zest and no leisure or pleasure. The passengers always scold him—hurl abuses at him sometimes. Being uneducated, the cab driver lacks manners and sense of self-respect too. At times, he is very rash and may cause an accident. Despite all these facts, he tries to be happy and carefree. As for his earning, it is never sufficient to support his family well. Moreover, continuous driving is more of a strain to the driver. We must be sympathetic towards the cab drivers and treat them with a sense of respect.

(*142 words*)

SUMMARY :

The life of a cab driver is very hard. He works the whole day. He knows no rest and is very poor. He gets a rough treatment from passengers and is himself ill-mannered too. Still he is happy. We should treat him with sympathy.

(*45 words*)

TITLE   : *Life of a Cab driver*

TEST YOURSELF

1.   A great part of Arabia is desert. Here there is nothing but sand and rock. The sand is so hot that you cannot walk over it with your bare feet in the daytime. Here and there in the desert are springs of water that come from deep down under the ground—so deep that the sun cannot dry them up. These springs are few and far apart, but wherever there is one, trees grow tall and graceful, making a cool green, shady place around the spring. Such a place is called an oasis. The Arabs who are not in the cities live in the desert all the year round. (**109** *words*)

SUMMARY :

....

....

....

....

TITLE : .... (*37 words*)

2. I remember that on a night during last winter there were several young girls of the neighbourhood sitting around the fire with my landlady's daughters and telling stories of spirits. When I opened the door, they broke off their talk. But the landlady's daughters told them that they must not fear me. I seated myself in a chair, took out a book from my pocket and pretended to read it. Actually I was hearing their stories. I heard one of the girls asking the others how long I had been in the room. She looked at me over her shoulder in such a manner that I could not stand her sullen gaze. I took the candle in my hand and went up to my own room.

(126 words)

SUMMARY:

....

....

....

....

TITLE : .... *(40 words)*

3. The master was serving food to the boys. The food got over. But Oliver, one of the boys, came forward with his plate and spoon in hand. He said to the master, "Please, sir, I want some more food."

"What !" said the master in a faint voice.

"I want some more food, sir," said Oliver again.

The master was mad with rage and aiming a blow at Oliver's head with the ladle said, "Do you want to be hanged ?"

"Why, sir ?" Shall we work while hungry ? Don't I deserve a fair meal even ?"

The master was dumb-founded. He had turned pale and words refused to come out of his mouth.

(111 words)

SUMMARY :

....

....
....
....
....

TITLE : .... *(37 words)*

4.   Soon after they came in sight of a body of Red Indians—all armed with weapons. The leader of the missionaries sent a man to them to proclaim that thye had no enmity with them. He simply wanted a passage through their country. But they started pelting stones, darts and arrows on the missionaries. So, his men attacked the Red Indians who held their ground for some time but then retreated. Missionary's men followed them with great zeal. Soon they found their way blocked into a narrow glen. So, they turned back to get out of the danger. But they came face to face with a large army of several thousands strong. The missionaries did not know what to do.   *(120 words)*

SUMMARY :

....
....
....
....
....
....

TITLE : ....*(40 words)*

27 PICTURE COMPOSITION

SPECIMEN:

THE MOUSE, THE FROG AND THE HAWK

Once there lived a mouse in a field near a village. His hole was near the village pond. He daily went to the pool to quench his thirst. There he met a frog and chatted with him daily. As a result, they became fast friends.

One day the frog, out of mischief, said to the mouse, "Don't you feel like swimming in the pool ?"

"Why not ; I like it very much. But I do not know how to swim."

"That doesn't matter at all. I shall tie your legs to my own leg. When I swim in the water, you will also swim with me."

The mouse agreed. Soon his legs were tied to the leg of the frog who swam about in the pond. He dragged the mouse with him merrily. The mouse was not used to a life in water. So, he was drowned and his dead body began to float on the surface of water.

A hawk saw the mouse's body floating and swooped down on it. He carried the mouse in his talons. Up went the hawk carrying the mouse. And lo ! the frog also went hanging down. Soon the hawk reached its eyrie (nest). He ate up both the mouse and the frog.

Moral : *Keep Company with Your Equals.*

TEST YOURSELF

Observe each of the pictures and write a readable story based on it :

1. THE BEE AND THE DOVE

SPECIMEN: 2. THE LION AND THE MOUSE

28 WRITING STORIES

Writing stories is an art just as telling stories is. A good story has the following features :

1. It has a good plot.
2. Its plot is developed through imagination to create interest.
3. It has the element of suspense at various stages.
4. Its language is simple, easy but impressive.
5. It has dialogues wherever possible. They enliven the story and bring it nearer real life.

Writing stories is a good exercise in written composition. It is easier than to writing essays because it has the elements of *interest* and *suspense*. Stories are written on the basis of the following :

1. A story based on a real happening in the past.
2. A story developed from an outline.
3. A story read in a book or heard from someone is reproduced.
4. A story is written after basing it on a *moral*.

HINTS FOR WRITING A STORY

1. A clear-cut idea of the plot should be made in mind.
2. The story should be started straightaway without any introduction.
3. The story should move in a natural way without any gaps.
4. Dialogues wherever possible, must be introduced in the story. They give the story a colour of naturalness.
5. The title of the story must be catchy and impressive.
6. The story must be written in the past tense. The language should be simple, correct and lively.
7. The outlines are generally given in the present tense but the story is to be written in the past tense. But the story must remain original to the outline. No new facts should be added.
8. A moral, if possible, must be given at the end of the story.
9: The story must end in a striking note to leave the reader impressed with the story.

1. THE DISHONEST HAND

Once upon a time a thief broke into the palace of a king. When he was breaking open a safe, the king woke up. He raised an alarm, "Thief ! Thief."

The thief got afraid and ran off. But some servants chased him and he was caught. He was given a sound beating and then handed over to the minister.

The thief was challaned and he was presented in the court. The minister asked the thief, "Did you break into the king's palace ?"

"Yes, my Lord ! I did, " replied the thief.

"Did you commit a theft there ?" asked the minister.

"No, sir, not at all."

"Who did it then ?" questioned the minister.

"It was my right hand, sir. It has become so wicked that it often commits thefts and brings me disgrace."

"You mean that you are innocent," asked the minister.

"By all means, sir. It was my right hand that made a hole into the safe and committed the theft," said the thief boldly.

"Then I won't punish you," assured the minister, "But your right hand is to blame. So, it will be punished."

"Thank you, sir," remarked the thief.

"Okay. I sentence your right hand to one year's *imprisonment*. It will serve the sentence inside the prison. You will stay outside," said the minister.

The thief was stunned at the words of the minister.

MORAL : *Cleverness is all right, but not over-cleverness.*

2. THE FARMER AND HERCULES

Once a farmer was going to a neighbouring town. He had loaded a cart with sacks full of wheat. The way had become muddy owing to rain.

Suddenly, one wheel of the cart sank into the soft mud and got stuck. The horse tried its best to get the wheel out of the mud but it could not do so. It heaved at it several times but all in vain.

The farmer himself remained inactive. He did not help the horse at all. On the other hand, he whipped it again and again. He asked several passers-by for help, but nobody paid any heed to his shouts.

Just at that time appeared an angel. He was Hercules, *god of strength*. He looked at the farmer begging the passers-by for help. He said to the farmer, "Why are you begging others for help ?"

"My cart has got stuck in the mud. I want it to be pushed out to the solid ground," replied the farmer.

"Did you yourself help your horse ?" asked the god.

"No, sir, I haven't."

"How can you expect others to do anything for you ?"

This question opened the eyes of the farmer. He put his shoulder to the wheel and made the horse exert. Lo ! the cart was on the hard dry ground in no time. The farmer was much too happy. He had learnt a useful lesson.

MORAL : *God helps those who help themselves.*

3. THE CLEVER JESTER

Once there was a king who had a very cheerful nature. He had a jester at his court who kept the king and his ministers in good mood. All of them liked his jokes. So, he came in the good books of the king. This success of the jester went to his head and he began to behave rudely with the nobles of the court. By doing so, he was taking undue advantage of the king's kindness.

One day the jester cut a very indecent joke with one of the ministers. He took it ill and complained against him to the king. The king also felt annoyed at the rudeness of the jester and decided to punish him. The jury of ministers prevailed upon the king and asked him to sentence the jester to death. Though unwilling, the king had to declare the death sentence for the jester.

The jester begged the king and the nobles for mercy. At first, nobody was ready to have mercy on him. But at last, one minister begged the king to allow him one concession. So, the king said, "Well, I cannot change the sentence at all. But I can allow you to choose the manner in which you like to die."

The jester was very clever and wise. So, he at once said, "My Lord ! I want to die a death of old age. I do not want to die while young."

The king and his nobles burst into laughter. They were so pleased at his wit that all of them decided to pardon the jester. So, he was let off though with a warning.

MORAL : *Wisdom beats strength.*

TEST YOURSELF

A. Develop the following outlines into a story :

1. A soldier walking through a market....sees a man selling caged birds....approaches him....buys all the birds....sets them free....people think him to be mad....all laugh at him........asks them the reason.....they ask why he had freed all the birds.....replies that he has been a prisoner of war......knows the suffering of slavery.

2. There is a dispute between the Sun and the Wind.....they decide to contest.....see a traveller......choose to try their strengths on him.....the Wind tries first.....blows hard.....the traveller clasps his cloak tighter.......then the Sun shines bright......the traveller takes off his cloak.....the Sun wins.

3. Two friends going on a journey.....promise to help each other.....a forest across the way.....reach its heart......a bear comes......one runs to climb up a tree......the other a fat fellow....lies down.....feigns death.....the bear sniffs him....thinks him to be dead.....leaves him and goes away.....the thin fellow comes down.....asks his friend what the bear said......he gives a curt reply....

4. A camel and a jackal are friends....jackal sees a melon field across the stream....suggests to the camel to enjoy melons.....camel agrees.....carries the jackal on its back....jackal soon satisfied.....begins to howl.....the camel forbids him to do so...."It is my habit", says the jackal.....farmer comes......beats the camel.....return journey.....camel dives mid-stream....jackal requests not to do so...."It is my habit," says the camel.....jackal is drowned.

5. A dark night....a blind man with a lamp in hand....two men laugh at him....what use is the lamp....blind man laughs back....lamp is for fools....they are careless....would not notice me in darkness.

6. A tiger lying under a tree....monkey sitting on the top notices the tiger.....insults.....tiger pays no heed....monkey angry......insults the tiger further.....tiger still quiet.....at last tiger gets ready to leave......have I insulted you, asks monkey.....not you, height but of the tree insulted me, says the tiger.

B. Write a story based on each of the following morals :

1. No pains, no gains.
2. Pride goes before a fall.
3. Union is strength.
4. Will finds the way.
5. A stitch in time saves nine.

C. Write a story with each of these famous titles :

1. The Wise Pigeons
2. The Wolf and the Lamb
3. The Leopard and the Traveller
4. The Fox and the Clever Rooster

29 WRITING ESSAYS

An essay is a regular well-connected written piece dealing with one topic/subject. An essay has three essential parts :

1. Introduction   2. Body   3. Conclusion

INTRODUCTION
It introduces the essay, *i.e.* begins it. It should be brief and to the point. It hints at the key-note of the essay. It is better to begin an essay with a popular proverb or saying if possible. It serves as the foundation of the essay.

BODY
The **body** of an essay is its main part. It deals with the salient facts, ideas, illustrations, *i.e.* examples and the personal views of the writer also. It must be written in well-framed sentences that are connected to one another in a logical manner. It must not be a collection of ideas but they must be written and explained in a chain based on proper grading and logical reasoning.

CONCLUSION
The **conclusion** of an essay should be striking but brief. The end must come in a natural manner. It should not be abrupt.

TYPES OF ESSAYS
There are four types of essays as under :

1. Descriptive   2. Narrative   3. Reflective   4. Imaginative

We dealt with descriptive and narrative essays in our previous classes. In this chapter, we shall study how to write reflective and imaginative essays.

1. ENVIRONMENTAL POLLUTION

Environment is very important for all living-beings—men, animals and plants. We are living in an age of science. Road vehicles are very common these days. They are run using petrol. Petrol fumes let out by vehicles are the biggest source of pollution. Factories are there in every region these days. The smoke let out by factory chimneys is the other big source of the pollution of **air**.

Besides **water** is also being contaminated in various ways. The sewage from house latrines is the biggest source of the pollution of water. Factories also dump their wastes and chemicals in the nearby water-bodies.

The third thing being polluted is the **food**. *Pesticides* are being used to keep the pests away from the crops. These pesticides are chemicals that pollute our food-sources if used carelessly.

Thus the three things that are our basic needs, are being polluted constantly. As a result, pollution of the environment has become a problem.

Noise has also increased a lot. Rash use of loud-speakers in religious places, marriages, festivals etc. and high-pitched advertisements in T.V. are chief sources of noise.

Clearly our environment has come to be polluted a lot. The future of living-beings is in danger indeed. To add to all these things, forests are being cut carelessly for wood, fuel and other things—*gums, resins, tree-bask,* etc. This deforestation has made the problem of pollution more serious.

The most effective method of fighting environmental pollution is to stop cutting forests and to plant new trees. Plants let out oxygen and keep the air fresh and fit for breathing. In their absence, the amount of carbon dioxide in the air increases and it becomes unfit for breathing.

Water can be kept safe from pollution by treating the sewage water scientifically before it reaches the rivers. Also, the factories should be warned against dumping their wastes into nearby water-bodies.

Noise can be prevented by banning the undue use of loud-speakers and asking the T.V. authorities not to allow advertisements with shrill sounds to be televised.

2. AUTOBIOGRAPHY OF A DOG

Hello students ! I am a pet dog kept by a rich man who is a lover of dogs. I have a keen desire to tell about my past. I think you will listen to it patiently and with interest. Here is my autobiography.

I was born in a kennel along with my brother and sister in the house of a rich man. He had kept my mother as a pet. So, there was great rejoicing when we were born. I still remember the face of my mother, though I can't recognise my brother and sister even if I meet them.

My mother loved me very much and so did her master. When I was only one month old, a friend of my mother's master came to his house. He took a liking for me and asked the rich man for me. So, I was handed over to him. This man is my present master and I am really proud of having such a kind man as my master.

My master brought me home and showed me to his wife, my present mistress. She was equally fond of me and treated me with love and kindness. I have always been looked after well. Timely baths, cleanliness of my body, regular nutritious food, morning and evening walks—all these I get from my masters.

As for me, I have served my masters most faithfully all my life. At night I become even more watchful. I do not bark at strangers unnecessarily. But God has given me a keen sense to tell a gentle stranger from a bad one. If I get suspicious of a person, I bark at him/her in such a frightful manner that he/she thinks of running away from there at once.

My master has a good business. He takes me for a morning walk along the canal. When he leaves for office, I see him off waving my right paw. When he comes home in the evening, I welcome him with a *loving whine*. He pats me and strokes my back. I pray to God daily for two things.

1. May my masters enjoy all His gifts !
2. Enable me to repay the love of my masters faithfully even if I have to give my life for them.

3. A PICNIC

We are living in an age of competition. Life is much too busy for everyone. Truly speaking, times are so hard that one has no time to stand and stare. So, relaxation and fun are much more needed now than they were needed earlier. Moreover, town life has become very artificial. Most of the time is spent in electric lights and in closed rooms. Man has got cut off from nature. So, outdoor fun is no less than a boon—especially in towns. Picnics are a good means of outdoor fun indeed.

Last Sunday, our family went for a picnic at the river-side. We have a car of our own. My mother and sister Julia cooked several dishes for the picnic. We packed our things and placed them in the car. Then we, a family of five, sat in the car and drove to the river-side.

In about an hour, we reached the river-side. After parking the car, we chose a suitable place to sit on. It was overgrown with green grass and was quite neat and clean. So, we placed our things there and spread a mat to sit on.

I, my sister and my younger brother played on the grass with a ball. We were much too happy to be away from the noisy world of the town. It was so calm and quiet on the river-side. A cool breeze was blowing. It touched the body and felt so soothing. My mummy and papa kept strolling along the river-bank.

At about 2-30 p.m., we had our lunch and lay down for the mid-day nap. Having had our rest for about an hour, we were up again. We enjoyed swing-rides on the swing that had been put up in the grassy lawn. At about 4:00 p.m., tea was prepared and we had it with *biscuits*. Then enjoying ourselves a lot for an hour more, we left for our home At about 6:00 p.m. we were back home quite happy and refreshed.

TEST YOURSELF

A. Write an essay on each of the following :

    (a) 1.   My Role Model   2.   The Book You Like Most
          3.   School Games   4.   Space Travel
          5.   A Robbery in a Train   6.   The Cyber Revolution

(b)	7.	Good Manners	8. If I were a Millionaire
	9.	Grow More Trees	10. A Visit to a Circus Show
	11.	My Favourite Game	12. Adventure in a Space craft
	13.	My Country	14. Importance of Games

B. Answer the following questions :

1. What is an *essay* ? How many parts has it ?
   ....
   ....

2. Write short notes on the three parts of an essay :

   (a) ....
   ....
   ....
   ....

   (b) ....
   ....
   ....
   ....

   (c) ....
   ....
   ....
   ....

3. How many kinds of essays are there ? Name them.
   ....
   ....

   1. ....
   2. ....
   3. ....
   4. ....

30 WRITING DIALOGUES

A *dialogue* is a conversation between two people. Dialogues are written using colloquial language. Remember that colloquial language has a good use of *contractions*. Precautions to be observed while writing a dialogue are as under:

1. Write *naturally* and *informally*.
2. Make a good use of *conversational language*.
3. Make a good use of *contractions* and *exclamations*.
4. There must be a *logical link* between *parts of the conversation*.

A SPECIMEN DIALOGUE

Between the *Ant* and the *Cricket* :

Cricket	:	Hello, Miss Ant ! how are you ?
Ant	:	Hello, Mr Cricket ! how do you do ?
Cricket	:	I am fine, Miss. You know I am a happy-go-lucky fellow. I believe in enjoying life.
Ant	:	Of course, it looks so.
Cricket	:	But why can't you find time to relax and enjoy yourself ?
Ant	:	Why ! I'm quite happy with my life.
Cricket	:	You are always busy carrying food to your nest; how is it ?

Ant	:	That is a way with us—ants. We can't sit idle. That is why we never beg anyone for anything.
Cricket	:	I think you labour much more than you need to do.
Ant	:	No, never ; you are mistaken, I think.
Cricket	:	Look at me. I pass most of the time singing merrily. I am also living my life after all.
Ant	:	May God keep you happy ! Okay ; bye. I am getting late for my work.

(Months pass. Winter sets in.)

Cricket	:	Tap, tap *(knocks at the door)*
Ant	:	Who is there ? *(opens the door partially)*
Cricket	:	It is me, Miss ! do you recognise me ?
Ant	:	Why not ; you are the happy-go-lucky Cricket. What can I do for you ?
Cricket	:	I need something to eat. I am very, very hungry.
Ant	:	Why ? Didn't you store food for winter ?
Cricket	:	No, Miss ; I was silly enough to sing the entire summer away.
Ant	:	Then dance the entire winter away. It will satisfy your hunger.
Cricket	:	Have mercy on me, Miss; I've been without food for two days.
Ant	:	Excuse me, Mr. Cricket. We ants never borrow or lend.

TEST YOURSELF

A. Develop a dialogue between a shopkeeper and a customer. The shopkeeper has given him a short measure. The customer is paying him less money. Base the dialogue on the story—*The Biter Bit*.

Customer	:	What is the cost of one burger ?
Shopkeeper	:	....
Customer	:	....
Shopkeeper	:	....

Customer	: ....
Shopkeeper	: ....
Customer	: ....
Shopkeeper	: ....
Customer	: ....
Shopkeeper	: ....
Customer	: ....
Shopkeeper	: ....
Customer	: ....
Shopkeeper	: ....
Customer	: ....

B. Develop short dialogues between :

1. two students after the declaration of the result
2. two friends after they have watched a film together.
3. a father and a son who is careless of his studies and wastes his time in play.
4. a teacher and a student who has not done his homework.

31 WRITING LETTERS

We have already read about the parts of a letter. They are—
1. beginning 2. Salutation 3. Body 4. Ending

Broadly speaking, there are two main types of letters :
1. Informal Letters   2. Formal Letters

FORMAT OF INFORMAL LETTERS

1. *Writer's address* :   14, Rue Schaffersen, Paris
2. *Date*   April 1, 2008
3. *Salutation*   My Dear Uncle,
4. *Body*   ....
                         ....

5. *Subscription*   Yours affectionately,
6. *Signature*   James

FORMAL LETTERS

1. *Writer's address*   E-1/18, Coles Park
                         James Street, Great Britain
2. *Date*   May 12, 2008
3. Address of the   The Telegraph Officer
   person or firm   128/D, Church Street
   receiving the letter Bristol, UK
4. Salutation   Dear Sir/Madam,
5. Body   ....
                         ....
                         ....

6. Subscription   Yours sincerely,
7. Signature   Perry

213

SPECIMEN LETTERS

1. Letter to younger brother on a bad report from his teacher.

74th Street, 199 Jackson Heights

New York, USA

8th February, 2008

Dear Nicholas,

I have just received a report from the teacher of your school about your result in the previous examination. It is satisfactory as far as your subjects of English and French are concerned. But in Science, History and Mathematics, you have not fared well. You need to put in more hard work in these subjects.

The general remarks from your teacher are disappointing too. He is displeased at your general conduct. His opinion cannot be wrong. He is really a noble person. I have profound regard for him as I, too, have been his student.

Nicholas, it is high time for you to mend yourself. If you have any bad company, give it up at once. Next time, I must get a good report about you. I am not going to tell daddy about this report. But if you do not mend your ways, I shall be forced to tell him everything.

Yours affectionately,

Thomas

2. Letter to a friend apologising for not having been able to attend his brother's wedding.

180 Oakdale Avenue

Down Town, Houston, USA

12th September, 2008

Dear Chris,

I am sure you will excuse me for not having been able to attend the wedding of your brother. It happened because of some circumstances beyond my control. Because of continuous rains, our street was flooded. There was water and water everywhere. Drain No. 8 had come to have a breach and its water marooned the area. We were completely cut off from the rest of the city for about a week.

Please accept my heartiest congratulations. Also, convey them to your brother, mummy and daddy.

Yours sincerely,
Michael

1. **Write a letter to the manager of the Milk Society about the bad quality of milk supplied.**

J-144, Victoria Street
Paris
Dated April 15, 2008

To
The Manager
Peterson Milk Society
James Street, Paris

Sir,

We are buying milk daily from a booth that supplies milk produced by your society. The milk supplied to us used to be the best. Unfortunately, it is not so now. The milk supplied at present is not pure. The supply is also not regular. Sometimes, it does not come at all and we have to go without milk. Therefore, be kind enough to take necessary steps to supply good quality of milk to us regularly.

Thanking you,

Yours faithfully,

David.

TEST YOURSELF

1. Write a letter to your younger brother advising him to be more careful in spending his pocket-money.
2. Write an application to your principal requesting him to exempt you from school games for a month.

3. Write a letter to your father requesting him to increase your monthly allowance.

4. Write a letter to your principal suggesting ways to improve spoken French in your school.

5. Your postman is very irregular and irresponsible in delivering your letters. Write a letter of complaint to the local postmaster.

6. Your neighbour's child has been missing since three days. Write a complaint to the Police Officer asking him to look for the child.

7. Your car has been stolen from a theatre. Write a complaint to the police.

8. Write a letter of advice to a friend who complains that he does not know how to spend his spare time.

9. Write a letter to the editor of a newspaper about the necessity of opening a post-office in your locality.

10. It is a fortnight to your examination, and you are unprepared. Write to your friend about your difficulty.

11. Write a letter to the editor of a newspaper expressing your views on the importance of imparting Moral Education in schools and colleges.